Piers Morgan:
The Classic Interviews

Piers Morgan:
The Classic Interviews

with John Sachs

JOHN BLAKE

Published by Blake Publishing Ltd,
3, Bramber Court, 2 Bramber Road,
London W14 9PB, England

www.blake.co.uk

First published in paperback in 2006

ISBN 1 84454 202 5

British Library Cataloguing-in-Publication Data:

A catalogue record for this book is available from the British Library.

Design by www.envydesign.co.uk

Printed and bound in Great Britain by Bookmarque Ltd

1 3 5 7 9 10 8 6 4 2

Papers used by Blake Publishing are natural, recyclable products made from wood
grown in sustainable forests. The manufacturing processes conform to the
environmental regulations of the country of origin.

Every attempt has been made to contact the relevant copyright-holders,
but some were unobtainable. We would be grateful if the appropriate
people could contact us.

For those who keep our secrets secret –
you know who you are!

EDITOR'S NOTE

These interviews, conducted in the late 1980s, are from the heyday of British Tabloid Journalism, when Piers Morgan's Bizarre column represented the cream of reporting on the stars. Piers possessed, and indeed possesses, a rare gift at getting well-knowns to speak frankly and revealingly about just what the public are interested in hearing. These timeless interviews have been left unaltered and are a testament to the fact that, in the fame game, some names will always live on, some will not. Some of the candidates have now sadly passed away, some have moved on to greener pastures, while others have withdrawn from the spotlight.

As a social document, the pieces reveal the everyday

lives of a variety of the rich and famous, detailing their pastimes, annoyances, loves (some now lost and replaced, you will notice), ambitions and dreams. From our perspective today, it is fascinating to observe what has unfolded between then and now and to be reminded of who and what was on the tip of everybody's tongue, often making what we still consider to be the recent past seem like a different era. There's something in here for everyone who lived during the eighties and nineties – a wonderful excuse to bask in the odd nostalgic moment and be reminded of the times we all lived through in this ever-changing world of fame.

FOREWORD

I have known John Sachs since our days together on Capital Radio when his voice, which currently thrills listeners with its depth and resonance, was a mere falsetto.

He has gone on to great success as a grown-up and has always been a pleasure to do business with; in fact, the only thing I can find to say against John is that he is too tall. Shortness is a quality I admire in a man.

Many pains and quite a few liberties were taken to produce this book. The quality of John and Piers's research has matched the stature of their subjects, and the result is a series of absorbing portraits.

Their earlier book, *Private Files of the Stars*, is

rumoured to have sold a copy, and I am sure this one will do just as well.

Michael Aspel

ACKNOWLEDGMENTS

To the BBC for their help and valuable time.

To our manager John Miles, for his advice and help.

Thanks to all the agents who helped us pin down a lot of these elusive butterflies: Jo Gurnet, International Artists, Emma and Tim Blackmore at Unique, Peter Powell (Hi, mate!), Tessa La Bar, Norman Murray, Mervyn O'Haran, Addison Cresswell and all the team at 'off the kerb', Gary Farrow, Peter Bennett-Jones, Clifford Elsen, Russ Lindsay, Neil Reading and anybody else we may have overlooked.

Thank you to everyone who worked on the book, particularly John Blake, who can spot a best-seller at a hundred yards.

And, of course, the biggest thank you to all the stars who were so helpful, co-operative and just a pleasure to talk to.

CONTENTS

INTRODUCTION

When Piers and John asked me to take part in this book, I was determined they would find out NOTHING about my life that everyone didn't already know. Then, before I could stop myself, I was telling them about the caning I got for illicit gambling at school, my first stumbling kiss with Maxine Stevens when I was 12, how I disgraced myself by throwing up at a family wedding, survived a car crash in Los Angeles and a tornado in Mexico, and enraged Sarah Miles in my worst ever interview. All I can say is that, if they got me to reveal MY most shocking secrets, God help the rest of the stars in the book!

Jonathan Ross

RUSS ABBOT

FULL NAME:
Russell Roberts.

NICKNAME:
Robbo when I was at school, Rusty, Skinny, Lanky all that kind of stuff, now I get called Baldy.

BORN:
On 8 September 1947, in Chester, a Virgo. My wife and two older boys are all Virgos. Dad was Donald Roberts, mum Elizabeth. Five brothers, John, Donald, Derek, Stewart and Neil.

SCHOOL:

First was Holy Newton Primary School in Chester, then I passed the 11 plus to Chester City Grammar School. I did OK, until I joined a band as a drummer. That ruined my academic career because I was always gigging the night before exams. My best subject was truancy, then maths and English and sport – soccer, gymnastics and cricket. I remember my dad catching me playing truant when I was walking to my mate's house. I saw Dad's car coming towards me, then it stopped. I told him a boy had been off sick and I'd been sent to pick up his homework. He said he would take me there – to Brook Lane where I said he lived. Eventually, I admitted I was lying, that I was playing truant. He said he knew all along and the lying had made it worse. He took me to see the headmaster and said he would leave him to deal with me. I got six of the best and thought, 'Thanks, pal.' It hurt him, but not as much as me.

JOBS:

I had a paper round and a Saturday grocery job which paid 10 shillings a week for an 8 a.m. to 6 p.m. shift. I got married in 1967 when I was just 19 and had to provide. Unfortunately, my band, The Black Abbots, didn't make enough for us to survive on, so I was forced to do loads of jobs. I worked at Hepworths on

Saturdays, folding suits, and at Bollands Butchery Bar on the biscuit counter. These old ladies would ask for broken biscuits and, if there weren't any there, I'd drop a bag for them and sell them for half-price. An accident of course.

GREATEST MOMENT:

Winning the Comedian Of The Decade award was great. And my West End debut in *Little Me*, the Neil Simon musical, was a thrill because it was so challenging playing nine roles with 21 costume changes. That was probably the highlight of my career.

COCK-UP:

I hosted the Lawrence Olivier awards live on TV with Julia McKenzie and this guy came up to accept an award for Best Comedy Performance in a West End play. I had prepared a joke about me coming fifth – but he made a very moving speech about a friend who had recently passed away. I wasn't listening and went ahead with my failure gag, mock tears and everything. I was met with total, embarrassed silence. I only found out why afterwards – I felt awful.

CARS:

My first car was a Hillman which cost me £20 and which I had for a day. It was handpainted pillbox red, brush-stroked like an oil painting. I went pub-crawling a bit to show it off to the lads but I noticed my bum was getting wet. After a few hours, the whole thing was soaking. Then I put the hood up and there was just a frame, no hood. I took it back the next day and got £15 back! Now I have a Mercedes.

HOME:
By the golf course in Wentworth with Bruce Forsyth, Sandy Lyle and Trevor Francis for neighbours. It's handy for golf and for work. My handicap is 12.

HOLIDAYS:
I like golfing holidays now in Florida, and lazing on the beach in the Caribbean.

FOOD:
Sunday roast, beef or lamb, and a good pasta.

DRINK:
Chilled white wine, and the occasional Scotch and water as a nightcap.

MUSIC:
Everything from Queen to Status Quo, Pink Floyd, Johnny Mathis and Paul McCartney. First record was Emile Ford's 'What Do You Want To Make Those Eyes

At Me For'. My favourite album would be a mixed collection of love songs. My favourite singers are McCartney and Mathis – probably Johnny best of all.

ADMIRE:
Tommy Cooper was brilliant – my role model in many ways.

HEIGHT:
6ft 2in.

FILM:
All The President's Men and *Marathon Man*.

FIRST KISS:
I was very young and didn't like it because it didn't taste very nice.

FIRST BONK:
I can't remember which magazine I was looking at!

MICHAEL ASPEL

FULL NAME:
Michael Terence Aspel, oddly enough, Wogan and I are both Michael Terence.

NICKNAME:
My mum called me Licky Dripping. My mum, Vi, comes out with all these centuries-old characters' names – I'm not quite sure why.

BORN:
I was born at my grandmother's flat in Battersea, South London – ten yards from Clapham Junction station.

SCHOOL:

My first school was Waldron Road Elementary in Earlsfield, South London. I used to get into trouble then. I was whacked by my father, though I'd never hit my own kids, and that made me a bit of a fighter. I had a fierce temper and was constantly assailed by the local kids. I was the champion after bashing up Billy White, the local bully. I reigned for quite a few months until Georgie Duckworth came along and relieved me of the title with a bit of nostril stretching. It was very honourable, squaring up and stuff. He gouged me a bit which was a bit off, and there was lots of hammering of the head and wrestling. I was eight or nine then and didn't mind losing – I'd had enough punch-ups. I remember my first day at my next school after passing the 11 plus. The day I arrived, I was made to feel very unwanted and unimpressive and I never quite recovered the self-confidence I'd had before that day. I left school when I was 16 after taking the school certificate and joined a publishing firm. My parents were very discouraging in my academic career and said that working-class people didn't go to university and that was that. Thus, I am not very bright.

JOBS:

I used to do a paper round, until the shop stopped

sending papers out. So I went round all the customers and said for threepence I would deliver them myself. That was more than they were paying the shop but I made a small fortune – enough to buy myself a bike. But I've never been any good as a businessman since. Twenty years ago, I did a teaching-aid thing and I was asked to read lessons on tape to these kids. I thought it was such a good idea that I put money into it. It was a maths tape – and I put a lot of cash into it. Within 18 months, I was left with all the debts and had to sell my house. It was heartbreaking because I'd spent 18 months doing this place up and never actually lived there. I've never tried anything since. I must be the only broadcaster of my age and experience and earning capacity who has no business interest. I have no production company, no nothing.

CAREER:

I started with Cardiff Radio when I was 21 – doing the voice of a children's hour villain called Captain O'Hagart· I was still working for a betting firm in Cardiff at the time and got the sack for doing the last episode against the boss's wishes! My first proper job was with the Welsh Repertory Company, earning ten bob a week. I was delighted! My first break in TV came in 1957 when I got a three-month contract as an announcer – which developed into newsreading and the *Miss World* contest. That was a difficult job. As you can imagine, it was very difficult to resist all those lovely girls. I did go out with one of the girls, Miss Uruguay. It was about 1965 and she was a 24-year-old girl called Hela Aguaray. We had a very nice time, then she went home. Some of the girls made it quite obvious they'd like to know me better. I remember Miss Sierra Leone accosting me in the lift and telling me she was 17. I said I was old enough to be her father and she replied, 'You are not too old, you are a lion who roars from within.' Then she told me I had a lovely voice, turned and kissed me full on the lips. It was quite a kiss, an amazing experience. As I recovered, she whispered that she was in Room 130 at the hotel. But, tempting though it was, I never followed it up. If the Mecca people had found out, we were both of the window.

GREATEST MOMENT:

Being a victim of *This Is Your Life*. I thought a) my family's been lying and b) who do I know in Australia? That was quite an experience. I was stunned by it – totally poleaxed. As far as interviews go, the most interesting person I've ever met would have to be Alan Alda, he was great. Michael Caine, as well, is always good. And I had the unique experience of seeing Margaret Thatcher frightened. She just did not want to do the chat show but her daughter Carol had reassured her it would be OK. She was fine once we started. The American actor Elliott Gould was impossible, my worst interview. His eyes glazed and his voice went and he didn't speak. It made good radio but he was a nightmare. Eventually, I sat there and refused to speak as well. It was great – total silence.

COCK-UP:

It came when I was doing *Miss World* at the Albert Hall in front of 27 million viewers and my mike packed in. I let it go and it swung between my legs in a very embarrassing way. The laughter lasted for three minutes. There was another terrible moment when I was attacked sexually by a German shepherd dog on TV. It took a good few minutes to drag it off. I also remember a phone ringing during a news bulletin and not being able to find it. It just rang and rang until someone discovered the phone in the bottom drawer.

CAR:

I drive a 1984 Mercedes 380 SL, which is great fun. I was driving a Porsche and these kids saw me and started chanting 'Yuppie'. Never again. My most shameful altercation came when I was driving. I had just joined Capital Radio and had a second-hand Alfa Romeo 1750. By my side was the most beautiful girlfriend and I wanted to go across Chelsea Bridge. Unfortunately, there had been roadworks and this man was standing in the middle of the road, reading a book, stopping traffic crossing the bridge. We stopped and laughed and I beeped him in a friendly way. But he was stroppy about it and said I couldn't go past, even though the roadworks had not actually begun and there was plenty of room. After an exchange of words, I drove round him on the pavement. But, as I did so, he kicked the car. To me that was like kicking my dog. I was out in a flash, hammering away at him – swinging punches like mad. It was a real old street brawl and I was very pleased with myself because his left ear was bleeding. I felt very ashamed afterwards, though, and I cringe when I look back on it now. But he deserved it at the time. He threatened to call the police, but I just got back into the car and drove off.

HOME:
I am the most despised species in the world – a middle-aged, middle-class, white Anglo-Saxon protestant living in the stockbroker belt of Esher, Surrey!

HOLIDAYS:
The Italian lakes. They hate middle-aged men there, which is great because everyone leaves me alone.

DRINK:

I used to drink whisky until it affected my personality and I started looking for dwarves and old ladies to beat up. Now I drink wine and Bollinger Champagne.

MUSIC:

I rarely listen to music. But, when I do, I adore jazz. The first record I bought was the *Hebrides Overture* by Mendelssohn. I can't think why.

HEIGHT:

5ft 9in and shrinking fast.

HOBBIES:

I like to draw and keep fit.

FAVOURITE FILM:

It's A Wonderful Life.

BOOK:

I like American novels like *Catch 22*. But probably *Ragtime* by E. L. Doctorow is my favourite.

HATES:

Other drivers more than anything else.

ADMIRE:

I would want to be John Mortimer or Peter Ustinov if I wasn't me.

FANCY:

I used to be in love with Ann Sheridan and Paulette Goddard was one of the sexiest women who ever lived. Of the latest crop, Glenn Close in *Fatal Attraction* was very attractive – women with big noses turn me on. She's had a nose job apparently, which astounded me. I like healthy hooters.

FIRST KISS:

My first meaningful kiss was with a girl called Margaret Parnell and I was 12 and deeply in love. It was disappointing because I knew that she wasn't keen at all and I suspected she was really in love with Jim Healy, my best pal. She's married and lives in Carshalton now.

FRIGHTENING MOMENT:

I was nearly killed in a car crash when I had a head-on collision with a lorry in a country lane. I had plenty of time to think about it which made it worse. But a far more scary moment was when a girlfriend of mine was in a difficult situation trying to end a relationship and asked me for help. I was sitting in this

Spanish cafe waiting for her to turn up and she never did, which started alarm bells ringing. I went up to where she had been telling him the bad news and it was sinisterly quiet. I was convinced he'd done her in and my body went freezing cold, though it was very hot. I was scared stiff. Luckily, everything was OK.

FIRST BONK:

I remember it well, because in the end she had to do it without me. No, seriously, I'd been through the army for two years as a virgin, which was dreadful, and when it did happen it lasted all of a second and I could have died happy having achieved it. The girl was very patient under the circumstances!

ROWAN ATKINSON

FULL NAME:
Rowan Atkinson.

NICKNAME:
I had several nicknames at school – Doopie was linked to the strangeness I sometimes displayed. Then I was Zoonie, Moon Man, Gruman and finally Greenie – all related to the supposition that I was in some way an alien force.

BORN:
I was born in Newcastle on 6 January 1955. My parents lived on a farm near Newcastle in the shadow of Consett steelworks. My mother wasn't at all happy about me going into showbusiness – she thought it was full of

cheques that bounced, homosexuals and nasty men in large velvet bow ties. She has since found out that not everyone wears bow ties, so her view has been modified. I am an absolutely perfect Capricorn – a complete loner, insecure and worried about myself. I'm a solitary fellow.

SCHOOL:
St Bees School, Cumbria. At school, I had a reputation for being slightly strange, a loner. I remember my headmaster giving me the only encouragement I ever really had to go into showbusiness. He called me into his office one day and said, although he had never in his life recommended a pupil to go into showbiz, he wouldn't disapprove if I gave it a try. I spent six years studying electrical and electronic engineering first at Newcastle then Oxford.

JOBS:
I wanted to be an electrical engineer. But when I applied to the BBC for an engineering job I failed miserably at the interview.

CAREER:
I was in plays at school – my first serious part was as Dauphin in Bernard Shaw's *Saint Joan* when I was 12. I seem to recall people laughing a lot but they probably found it more cute than funny. I stole Peter

Cook and Dudley Moore sketches wholesale for school reviews, then graduated to stealing Monty Python sketches at college. Then I teamed up with Richard Curtis and we wrote a lot of comedy which led to me being offered *Not The Nine O'Clock News*.

CAR:

Aston Martins. I also possess a Heavy Goods Vehicle licence – I enjoy driving.

MUSIC:

I've got a fairly catholic taste in music – from rock to classical.

ADMIRE:

I thought John Cleese was the funniest man in Britain for years before I met him – and now I have got to know him that opinion hasn't changed a bit. Apart from being very funny, he is a very good actor too. I also admired Peter Sellers very much – he is someone in whose footsteps I would like to tread. His character acting was brilliant and he was a workaholic who never said no to anything.

HOMES:

I was living in a small flat in Camden, when I walked down to Euston Station one evening, bought *Country*

Life, saw this house in it and bought it the next day. It's an 18th-century rectory in a little village outside Oxford, with five bedrooms, a two-bedroom cottage and five acres of ground including a tennis court. I can really relax there. I love pottering in the garden.

HOBBIES:
Electronics, truck driving, cars and drumming. My favourite occupation is washing the car, that to me is complete happiness. And I like vacuuming, and mowing the lawn.

AMBITION:
I would like to play the villain in a James Bond film – the one who sneaks up behind him and says, 'Not so fast, Mr Bond.'

FRIGHTENING MOMENT:
I had a nasty car crash in 1985 in Canada when the car turned over three times on the motorway. Apart from a few scratches, I was unhurt. I was a passenger – we were very lucky. I thought I was going to die – but all I could think about was how embarrassing it was going to be telling my friends about it and the inconvenience of having to find my way home. But it made me realise you have to live life to the full and not worry about things like pensions too much.

ROSEANNE BARR

FULL NAME:
Roseanne Barr.

NICKNAME:
Rosey.

BORN:
I grew up in Salt Lake City, the Mormon capital of America, among Holocaust survivors, 12 families given shelter by my grandparents who owned the tenement slum I lived in. When I was only three, I'd sing and dance to them to stop them all talking about the butchery they'd suffered. I rebelled against the Mormon Church when I was 15 and started drinking

beer, smoking cigarettes and begging a boy called Eric to have sex with me but he didn't.

SCHOOL:

I hated school – and couldn't wait to leave. I don't have any memories of it at all.

CAREER:

I used to work in a coffee shop where all the men made wisecracks about my body. I used their gags to write material for sketches. Eventually, I was at a place called The Comedy Works, where this comic did a routine slagging women. I was furious and got up on stage to have a go at him. I went down so well I became a regular and I ended up with my own TV show, *Roseanne*.

FRIGHTENING MOMENT:

Falling pregnant at 17 when I was unmarried and the father didn't want to know. I wanted to keep my baby, Brandi, but I couldn't afford anything better than a cockroach-infested hole, so I eventually gave her to the Jewish Family And Children's Service. The day they took her I promised to see her again when she was 18. And I did – I hired a private detective to find her and we get along great now.

GREATEST MOMENT:
The birth of my children, each time it was wonderful.

CAR:
I drive a Mercedes Sports.

HOME:
I live with my second husband, Tom Arnold, in a £1,200-a-month rented apartment in Encino, California. We have a black-bottomed swimming pool and everything. [Editor's note: Roseanne Barr is now divorced]

HOLIDAYS:
The Caribbean.

FOOD:
I used to weigh just 7st 7lbs as a teenager – then I decided to really pig out on junk food and be happy. My weight doubled in two years. I'm fat and I'm proud of it. If anyone asks me how my diet is going, I say, 'Fine, how's your lobotomy?' I weigh 16st 4lbs now and gorge myself silly on peanuts. And I feel sexy now I'm so fat.

DRINK:
Beer, especially lager – and white wine.

HEIGHT:
5ft 2in.

HATES:
Bette Midler. If I see her ugly face again, I'm gonna slap her 'til her eyeballs spin. And I hate Hollywood – it's a back-stabbing scum-f*****, small-minded town.

HOBBIES:
Watching TV, reading, talking, listening to music and having sex with my husband.

AMBITION:
I would like to make a lot more films, Woody Allen-type movies with lots of black humour. But my greatest ambition is to be happy – isn't everyone's?

FRIGHTENING MOMENT:
For a joke as a 16-year-old teenager, I put a blanket on my head and walked down the highway. I was hit so hard by a car that its bonnet embedded in my head and left me in a coma for four days. I needed skin grafts, the works – and at one stage I believe I actually died and went briefly to heaven. I went through a tunnel of light – the whole thing. It was frightening but wonderful. My parents put me in a mental institution for eight months afterwards because I

started having nightmares, thinking I was being buried alive. I was drugged up most of the time but the nuthouse made me think clearly.

FIRST BONK:

I was on a visit home from the nuthouse and this guy in the neighbourhood, Sandy, kept trying to have sex with me. He gave me some pot in his flat and suddenly his proposition seemed more interesting. We started having sex on the couch and I got really into it – he took me to the bedroom and we did the whole thing. It was great.

MICHAEL BARRYMORE

FULL NAME:
My real name is Michael Keiron Parker.

NICKNAME:
I was nicknamed Kier because everyone in my block of flats was called Michael, so 30 kids used to turn up when Mum shouted, 'Teatime!' I was called Branch, Stick and Bones quite a lot – even the local paper called me Bones Parker!

BORN:
4 May 1952 in a corner bedroom in a flat in Bermondsey, Docklands. Mum was Margaret and Dad was George. He was a compulsive gambler and a

drunk. He left home when I was 11 and I haven't seen him since. I used to make excuses to my schoolmates that he was a long-distance long driver. But I got teased quite a lot. I don't know where he is now.

SCHOOL:
St Joseph's Catholic School in the Docklands. I was taught by nuns who smacked us a lot on the back of the legs. We had to wear shorts, so it hurt. I couldn't wait to get out of school.

JOBS:
I had a paper round at ten, doing the *London Evening Standard* at night. And I would clean eight cars on a Saturday, charging £1.50 a car, so I did well. I once worked as a junior hairdresser to Ricci Burns. I helped him cut the hair of people like Candice Bergen, Lulu and Shirley Bassey.

CAREER:
I had a band called Fine China when I left school; we did Jethro Tull covers mainly. I was the keyboard player. But I always wanted to be a comedy actor. I went to Butlins as a Redcoat when I was 17, in 1969. Then I applied to the London Academy of Music and Dramatic Art when I was 19 and I won a three-year scholarship. But, before I could start, I entered a

talent contest in a local pub and I won because all my mates were there and the judges were scared they would be beaten up. So I never went to college – I went off to the clubs instead. I was promptly paid off everywhere I went, which made me realise what a mistake I'd made in not going to LAMDA. I only carried on because I didn't want people saying 'I told you so' for the rest of my life. My 'AWRIGHT' catchphrase started from the way South London people speak. A bit Ken Livingstone-ish. Everything was awright in the pubs and girlfriends were all tarts.

FRIGHTENING MOMENT:

I am not a nervous performer at all, I'm lucky like that. But my first Royal Variety show was scary. The trouble is that we are all in there together and it only needs one person to look scared and everyone starts trembling. I like to get away from everyone else. I'm not like I am on stage – no one could be that manic all the time.

CARS:

My first car was a Bubble Car which I paid a fiver for on a Friday. Now I have a Mercedes 500SL and a Bentley 8.

HOME:

I live between Essex and Hertfordshire – on the border.

HOLIDAY:

Best ever was when I rented a place in Palm Beach for a month last year. On the left was the Kennedy summerhouse and on the right was the Trump place! No one recognised me in my baseball cap, the weather was brilliant and we just cooked for ourselves and lay on the beach.

FOOD:

Italian, then Indian.

DRINK:

I don't drink alcohol at all, I drink Coke.

MUSIC:

I've recently got into opera, which I enjoy. My first record was 'My Boy Lollipop'. My favourite album would be *Your Song* by Elton John and my favourite singers would be Dusty Springfield, Paul Young and Rod Stewart.

BOOK:

Looking Through The Mirror Glass by Sidney Sheldon. It's a great book about a comic.

ADMIRE:

My idol is Jack Nicholson, he never looks as if he's

acting. He also has a similar hairstyle to me! I love Danny Kaye, Steve Martin and a new duo called God and Jesus are hysterical. They will be huge, I am sure of it. It's Oxbridge humour but very, very funny.

HEIGHT:
6ft 3in.

HOBBIES:
I collect old tin-plate toys. I don't have much time for hobbies, too busy with the career.

FILM:
Gypsy. Rosalind Russell was a tremendous performer.

AMBITION:
I've given up *Strike It Lucky*. I thought it was time I should be known for something else. I want to be alternative again, not so mainstream popular. The show was very good for me and they wanted to carry on with it but I wanted to move on. I have proved I can do it. My career comes before money. A new series for English TV is coming up. It's not a quiz show, it's more comedy. America is my main target now; I think they are looking for an English type of quiz show. It's going to be a busy few years, I hope. It's exciting, but I've come from nothing so if it happens again so what? I

could cope with that. I'd like to be in a film too, if I got the chance.

HATES:
People who stay in the middle lane on the motorway. They are so irritating.

FRIGHTENING MOMENT:
As a kid, we were mucking around on a bombsite and there was a wall still standing with a staircase. We all got on it and I was pushed off – landing 20 feet down on some sharp corrugated sheeting. It nearly slit my throat – very frightening.

FANCY:
Diana Ross. She was a lovely-looking girl.

FIRST KISS:
I was 11 and it was on the second-floor stairs in a block of flats. I can't remember her name. Me and my mates had to pick a name out of a hat and kiss that girl – I had a result!

FIRST BONK:
I was 16 when I had my first proper girlfriend; she was a 16-year-old German girl, one of the band groupies. I lost my virginity to her.

BEST PARTY:

We had a party for the end of a *Strike It Lucky* series and the producer poured some brandy over Cheryl, my wife, and then lit a fag and set her alight. He's done it twice, I won't let him near brandy now. He talks looking one way and pouring it the other way.

CILLA BLACK

FULL NAME:
Priscilla Maria Veronica White. My mum's name is Priscilla as well and she was always known as Big Priscilla, whereas I was Little Priscilla. I lived in a very tough area and to have a posh name like that was incredibly embarrassing. Luckily, the kids called me Cilla at school. The Black bit came when a local paper, called *The Mersey Beat*, had a misprint. They knew my surname was a colour and guessed wrong! My manager Brian Epstein quite liked it, though, and put it into my contract. My dad went spare because he didn't think any of his mates down at the docks would believe I was his daughter! They used to call him the Frustrated Minstrel because he didn't know whether he was black or white!

NICKNAME:

John Lennon used to call me Cyril, and Paul McCartney still to this day calls me Silly Cilla!

BORN:

I'm a Gemini. I was born at Stanley Hospital in Liverpool on 27 May 1943. My three brothers are George, John and Alan.

SCHOOLS:

My first school was St Anthony's R.C. I absolutely loved it. It was a very working-class school with 48 pupils and we had just one teacher, apart from the music tutor. I left school to do a year's commercial course.

JOBS:

My first and only job outside music was as a clerk typist for BICC, The British Instigated Calendar Cables Ltd. I handed my notice in after six months, after I passed my audition at EMI with The Beatles' producer George Martin. When they asked why I was leaving, I said, 'Because I'm going to be a star!'

CAREER:

I always sang at school, in the breaks, every spare minute. There used to be afternoon sessions at places like The Cavern – so we'd nip off from school to see bands like The Beatles and Rory Storm and The Hurricanes. All my mates used to egg on the guys and say, 'Go on, give Cilla a go, she can sing.' So they would let me, just to have some peace and quiet. I was asked to join the best group in Liverpool at the time called The Big Three – The Beatles were in Germany just then. Then I joined King Size Taylor and The Dominoes who were great. Taylor was 6ft 5in long and wide. Then John Lennon persuaded Brian Epstein to let me sing with The Beatles at The Majestic Ballroom in Birkenhead. I was bloody awful! I was very nervous, had never done an audition before and it showed. Brian wasn't very impressed and it wasn't until a year later that I sang again at the Blue Angel Club in Liverpool. Brian was in the audience and he came up afterwards to ask if he could sign me up. My first song was 'Love Of The Loved', which Paul McCartney had written for me. I was great mates with all The Beatles. Me and my mates were always mucking around with them. John was always saying, 'Come on, Cyril, let's see what you can do.' I keep in touch with the McCartneys but I'm a carnivorous eater so we don't get invited round that often! No, I'm joking. I remember them inviting me and Bobby to dinner in Barbados once and the food was delicious. Linda is a great cook. My son Robert is a great friend with Mary McCartney. But I'm not very good at keeping in touch – Ringo Starr and Frankie Howerd always have a go at me for never ringing them. But I don't like to be too pushy.

FRIGHTENING MOMENT:

I did a Ouija board with The Beatles once and George Harrison played a wicked practical joke on Paul McCartney. Paul's mother had died a while before and he loved her very much. George made out there was a message from Paul's mum Mary as we sat round the board. He said Mary reckoned their next single would be number 1 in the *NME* charts. Then Paul sussed it and said, 'Hang on, my mum died before the *NME* was even invented.' I felt very uncomfortable about the whole thing to be honest.

GREATEST MOMENT:

When Robert was born. It was the most marvellous thing – I honestly didn't think I could ever produce a child.

COCK-UP:

There have been so many! I remember doing a TV show in Southampton to plug my first single 'Love Of The Loved' in 1963. It was only my second time on TV and they told me to dance in the break. So I did – right past the camera. There was a blank screen for about ten seconds. That was very embarrassing. But we had some terrible cock-ups when I did my show for the BBC. We went into the street and saw if people recognised me. Here are some of the worst ones:

1) I was posing as the girl behind the counter at a Green Shield stamps shop and this woman came in and asked for an electric iron. Three times I came back with a shovel but she never said a word. Eventually, I got quite frustrated and said, 'Do you know who I am?' And she said, 'Of course, Cilla, how long have you been working here?' She thought this was my day job.

2) I was a petrol-pump attendant in a garage and this bloke recognised me straight away, so I asked him if he wanted me to dedicate a song to anyone. He said, 'Yes, "You're My World."' When I asked who he wanted to dedicate it to, he looked straight at the camera and said, 'HE'LL know who it's for.' I couldn't believe it – we couldn't use it, in them days people wouldn't have approved!

3) I was in the studio and we were sending the crew into people's houses. One day, I sent them into a prostitute's house by mistake and our man had to join a huge queue of fellas all waiting for their turn. It was live, so I said hastily, 'Oh, she's got a lot of relatives.' It turned out the girls were actually watching our show at the time. It got worse because one of the men was an Indian guy and I couldn't tell that from the studio.

I asked him if he'd just been on holiday, adding, 'You've got a nice tan.' When I realised what I had done, I was inconsolable. I rang Kenny Lynch the next day and asked him if he'd seen the show and been offended. He was the only one who told me the truth. Everyone else was saying nobody noticed, but he said he did and he had been offended.

4) We had a camera on a crane and we were talking to all these people in this block of flats. I spotted this couple, and told the camera to zoom in on them – at which point they disappeared inside. I shouted out, 'Come on, who are you with?' Eventually, the woman came out looking very worried because she was obviously with somebody she shouldn't have been with. It turned out her husband was in the pub watching all this on TV. It was terrible – I nearly got cited in the divorce case and sued for it. Another very embarrassing moment was when I went up to ask Albert Finney for his autograph in a restaurant and spilled the entire contents of me bag over his dinner. He wasn't best pleased!

CARS:
My first car was a Bentley, but I never drove it. I moaned to Brian Epstein that all The Beatles had a big Rolls, so he bought me one. But it never left the showroom and we lost £500 on it. I bought a Mini

instead, all fitted out! Now I have five cars. A Rolls, and a fleet of Renaults for the kids. I'm thinking of getting a Mini Cooper soon – far more practical.

HOME:
I live in Denham, Bucks. And we've just bought a two-bedroom flat in Westminster. The lift only goes to a certain floor then you have to have a key to get to our flat.

HOLIDAY:
I love the Seychelles, because I don't have to do the washing and cooking there. But we've got a smashing holiday home in Marbella that takes a bit of beating.

FOOD:
Chinese – I love that crispy aromatic duck.

DRINK:
Champagne, non-vintage Moet Chandon. I have a bottle a day.

MUSIC:
When I was 12, I went out and bought 'Why Do Fools Fall In Love' by Frankie Laine. Now my son Robert's into Jimi Hendrix, which is great because that is my era. But I prefer Whitney Houston.

ADMIRE:
The Queen, Margaret Thatcher, Mother Theresa. I love strong women.

HEIGHT:
5ft 6in and shrinking.

HOBBIES:
Trying to keep fit. I have a rowing machine, a running machine and a bike. I could charge people to use my games room. I tried jogging up and down the lanes but I felt awfully rude not stopping to talk to people.

FAVOURITE FILM:
When Harry Met Sally. A Fish Called Wanda – that's got everything.

AMBITION:
I would love to make it in America. It's been a bug-bear since I went there in 1965 when The Beatles played Shea Stadium. Brian got me a booking at the Plaza Hotel but it wasn't right. I was very homesick, after four weeks there. I was so miserable that I went home and never went back. I regret that now. I would love to do what I am doing now in the States, or a sitcom. I've always put my family first, and Jack is only 10, so I have to wait until his education is sorted out first. Maybe later on.

FRIGHTENING MOMENT:

In 1980, we were coming back from Liverpool in the Rolls when the road salters were on strike. We skidded every which way on the M1, and missed cars everywhere. We ended up facing the way we'd come – and the alternator wouldn't work, so we were stuck. Then we saw an AA van coming towards us and we thought, 'Great, we're OK.' But it didn't stop, and smashed straight into us. As it reached us, I shouted, 'God!' and threw myself against Bobby. It was like slow motion, absolutely horrible. I was convinced I'd end up either dead or in a wheelchair. But at the last minute the van skidded as well and ripped off the whole side of the Rolls – leaving us unharmed. It was an amazing escape really. What was even more incredible was that we had all these Christmas presents in the back – like china, videos and glass. But nothing broke.

HATES:

I hate smokers – what gets right up my nose is when I walk into a lift and someone starts smoking. But I never have the guts to say anything unless I'm in a restaurant, then I will cough very loudly.

FANCY:

I love Kurt Russell. I was asked to go on *Wogan* with

him but couldn't make it – I felt terrible. And I quite fancy Robert Redford, Tom Selleck and Kevin Costner.

FIRST KISS:

His name was Frank, he went to art school and I thought he was gorgeous. I remember it so well, but it was only a fleeting thing on the cheek. We had both fallen over and we were going to the nurse for treatment, and because we were from Liverpool we compared scabs. Bobby won't allow me to reveal more details!

FIRST BONK:

Bobby is the only man I have ever made love to. I didn't believe in sex before marriage – it was unheard of in my day. I met Bobby when I was 16 and he was 18, in the Zodiac Club. I thought he had money or he was foreign because he had a suntan. I went over with a friend and chatted him and his mate up. Then he spoke and told me his dad ran a confectioner's business. I thought, 'Thank You, God, not only does he have money and a tan, but he's also from Liverpool.' But, in fact, he worked on the sweets counter in Woolies and he'd just come back from a package holiday in Torremolinos. I was 25 when we got married. I went out with a few other men but they were boring compared to Bobby.

JULIAN CLARY

NAME:
Julian Peter McDonald Simon Clary.

NICKNAME:
I used the title Joan Collins Fan Club for years around the cabaret circuit and no one bothered with it. Then, when I went on TV, Joan's solicitors wrote to me saying, very politely, that, while they wished me all success in my career, could I please stop using her name. I was quite glad; it was getting to the stage where if she had been run over by a bus my career would have been over!

BORN:

25 May 1959 in Surbiton, Surrey – the home of *The Good Life*. My mum was Brenda McDonald and my dad was Peter Clary. I've also got two sisters, Frances and Beverley.

SCHOOLS:

I went to a prep school called Arundel House, then St Benedict's public school. I was best in the class at writing stories and enjoyed taking part in school plays. But I don't have very fond memories of my schooldays. People were always being beaten. I got whacked once for forgetting my swimming things. This teacher wafted in wearing clouds of black robes and told me to get up to his room. Then I leaned across his armchair and he really went for me. I got four whacks, and I'd just forgotten something, it was only human error. On another occasion, someone stole a teacher's strap and he said he'd beat all 300 of us if it didn't come back. Can you believe that he beat ALL of us with a cricket bat? The problem was that St Benedict's was run by monks and I was raised to feel a sense of guilt about everything. I liked to be rebellious so I would wear pink socks or splash on perfume to annoy the other boys. They wouldn't talk to me and I wouldn't talk to them so I ended up a fairly lonely boy!

JOB:

Nothing could beat the excitement of working in the photocopying room at British Gas with three women who had worked there for years. Their philosophy was to do as little as possible and, when people asked for a photocopy to be done, they would reply, 'Oh that's out of the question, we are snowed under with work, possibly by Friday week.' But the reason they were busy was because they were actually making their own clothes! They would all have their patterns out on the floor and I would keep watch. When I left, I started doing singing telegrams. I had to go to four parties a night, say poems, make whoopee noises – everything. I got paid £12, even though the agency charged £55. By the end I was doing Don Juans and Gay Tarzans mainly – it made me fearless.

CAREER:

When I was still at school, I joined Group 64, an amateur-dramatic group in Putney. My first starring role was in *Man For All Seasons*. Then I teamed up with a friend, Linda Savage, for a two-man cabaret show. That's when I started wearing make-up and stuff. We called ourselves Glad and May and performed in pubs in South London!

FRIGHTENING MOMENT:

I was on tour with my one-man show in Southend when this huge glitter ball fell down next to me. It crashed down from 20 feet above me and landed less than six inches away. I was in the middle of a song and there is no doubt it could have killed me – it was enormous and very heavy. I was so shocked I stopped singing and husked a few verses, made a few cracks about people dropping their balls, and recovered. All very un-nerving.

GREATEST MOMENT:

Playing my show at the London Palladium. It was brilliant, the place was sold out and it's such a beautiful venue. You get such a roar of laughter from 2,000 people. It was an unforgettable night.

COCK-UP:

The time when I spotted a man with his eyes shut in the front row and thought he was asleep. I made some very cruel jibes but he kept his eyes closed. Eventually, he said, ever so quietly, that he was blind. I also got into trouble when I used to raid women's handbags during my cabaret show. I found one letter that had hospital appointments for a woman who had a nipple disorder and read it out. She was actually a friend of mine and she hasn't talked to me since.

CARS:
My first car was a white Citroen 2CV special. Now I drive a new Toyota MR2, metallic blue.

HOME:
My first home was a flat in Surbiton, now I have a one-bedroom flat in Camden Town, North London.

HOLIDAYS:
The Maldives was like the Bounty adverts – just stunning. There was one restaurant and you paid the whole bill at the end of the trip. There was nothing to do except get desperately hot and swim in the beautiful sea. Everything slows right down.

FOOD:
I like Japanese food best, stuff like sushi.

DRINK:
I don't drink much alcohol, but if I had a choice it would be vintage Pink Champagne, I suppose.

MUSIC:
I listen to female country singers like Patsy Cline, Loretta Lynn and Tammy Wynette. The first record I bought was Marc Bolan's 'Ride A White Swan'. I was 11.

BOOK:
Portrait Of A Lady by Henry James.

HEIGHT:
6ft 2in.

ADMIRE:
I admire people who have been around for a while like Barbara Windsor, who still works bloody hard. She knows the business so well yet she is still not cynical. Paul Merton, the guy from *Whose Line Is It Anyway*, makes me laugh a lot and so do Victoria Wood, French and Saunders, Les Dawson and Ben Elton.

TV SHOW:
It wouldn't be comedy, probably something like *Life On Earth*.

FILM:
Gone With The Wind was one of the few films I didn't lose interest in before the end.

Hobbies:
Taking my dog, Fanny, for a walk, and cleaning. I find it therapeutic to wipe down the kitchen surfaces.

HATES:

I can't stand Steve Martin, and I hate officialdom, stupid men in uniforms whose job it is to give everyone a hard time. They used to ban me from bringing Fanny into shows – and she was the star.

AMBITION:

I would like to write a serious book, short stories, an autobiographical book to make people cry. I've made them laugh – I'd like to try the other way.

JOHN CLEESE

NAME:
John Cleese.

NICKNAME:
All my nicknames were based on variations of the word cheese – Old Cheese, Cheesey, Gorgonzola, Stilton. I thought Stilton Cleese would make a splendid old-fashioned theatrical name.

SCHOOL:
I was very shy and got bullied a lot in my first two years. I remember my father arriving to pick me up once and looking round and realising I was the boy two others were sitting on. My one and only

exchange of physical violence was with a fellow called John Darby. I still see him occasionally. It was one of those deep-seated resentments which boiled over. I think I lost; it was certainly stopped when I was getting the worst of it. I was about ten and it was at St Peter's School, Weston-super-Mare. I went on to Clifton School at 17 and had a good time – I got my three A levels and got in the cricket team and ran the house library pretty well, reorganising the card system. My friends used to vow to shuffle my cards up if I upset them. But then I got back one term and discovered I had NOT been made a house prefect. To arrive at that age and status and find I had not been made a prefect was really hurtful. Ever since then, I have felt totally derisive towards honours given to me – I think they are plain silly. It's like grown men going up to get the fourth-form reading prize. I hate awards and won't accept them. It all goes back to school.

GREATEST MOMENT:
I think my best memories are those little moments of exquisite happiness in very ordinary circumstances. I recall sitting in a deckchair in my garden reading a book I enjoyed, my two cats and two daughters were all playing in the garden and I remember looking at them and feeling complete happiness. I am deeply

suspicious of moments when everyone claps you. That's false to me, and shallow.

EMBARRASSING MOMENT:

A moment of divine embarrassment happened in 1969. I had written a film script and my agent recommended a director to me. He asked me to telephone this guy but I was just off to Majorca for a ten-day holiday and, when I rang, there was no reply. So I left it and, when I returned from my very nice jaunt in Majorca, I decided to ring this guy again. His lady friend answered the phone and I said hello and how delighted I was to hear the news about Mr X, referring to him wanting to see the script – and there was a long silence before she said very quietly, 'They buried him this afternoon.' I don't think you can have a worse moment than that, can you?

HOLIDAYS:

I went to Northern India and that was wonderful. The game reserves in Kenya were also fascinating, but I find that reading four books by the pool is equally satisfactory.

FILM:

I think *The Third Man*.

BOOK:
War And Peace.

MUSIC:
Flute music for when I feel peaceful, and something with good lyrics like Randy Newman for the livelier moments.

HATES:
I would say, at the moment, I am very aware of the number of people who pretend to know things when they don't. The moment I hear someone say, 'I really don't know much about this but I will say this much,' my heart warms to them. That is why I disliked Mrs Thatcher so much; I didn't believe she knew what she was talking about.

AMBITION:
I want to write, and spend time in my garden.

FRIGHTENING MOMENT:
I think getting in touch with my childhood experiences with a psychiatrist will live with me for a long time – it was a very scary thing.

MEN YOU ADMIRE:
I admire people for ten years, then go off their work.

But I consistently admire Robert Bolt. Also, Michael Frane as a writer and a person. And Jonathan Miller has done very good work for 30 years. Of the actors, Kevin Kline and Bill Hurt would be my favourites.

WOMEN YOU ADMIRE:
It's varied, started with Doris Day, and passed through the classier ones like Ingrid Bergman, and the more outrageous ones like Gina Lollobrigida. Recently, I thought Jamie Lee Curtis was unbelievably beautiful. In a certain light, she looked amazing. Julia Roberts, too, is adorable.

FOOD:
Fish, pasta, good veg.

DRINK:
I like French wine and sparkling mineral water and I actually do drink a lot of Schweppes tonic. I'd been drinking it for years before they asked me to do the ad – that tickled me.

BEST PARTY:
Graham Chapman's memorial service was the only occasion I've been at which succeeded 100 per cent in what it was trying to be. It was a wonderful day,

which was absolutely what Graham would have enjoyed himself.

FIRST KISS:

I was unbelievably old – it was a very good experience and I enjoyed it a lot. I was in my early 30s, I think, much older than I would like to admit.

FIRST BONK:

It was at the Station Hotel. It didn't put me off, it certainly wasn't repellent or embarrassing or awful but more surprising. You can read about it but, when it comes to it, you don't really have any idea what it's all about.

MICHELLE COLLINS

FULL NAME:
Michelle Daniella Collins.

NICKNAME:
I've never had one.

BORN:
28 May 1963. I'm a Gemini.

SCHOOL:
Yerbury Junior School and Highbury Hill Girls Grammar School. We used to go on great school trips – the best one was to Italy, where we were constantly chased by young soldiers. We pretended we were

Catholics so we could go to midnight mass and get out! Little did Miss Butcher know what we were up to. My worst memory is having to wear Clark's shoes – my feet were a size seven so they looked like boats.

JOBS:
My first acting job was in a video for Squeeze called 'Up The Junction'. I was the girl from Clapham who got up the duff.

CAREER:
I used to go to Cockpit Youth Theatre, then did a drama course at Kingsway Princeton College. After that, it was loads of fringe work, answering ads in *The Stage* and that sort of thing. It was sheer hard work, determination and NO nepotism!

FRIGHTENING MOMENT:
My first day at *EastEnders*. I thought I knew everyone because I'd watched the show on TV for so long. That was a very strange and nervous feeling. My first scene was with Nick Berry and he was great to me. He really made me feel better. And Linda Davidson was nice too; she played the punk girl Mary and she was leaving that day. She gave me one good bit of advice – don't do it! No, she was great. Also, my first interview with Sting on *The Word* – I was terrified, though he was very kind.

GREATEST MOMENT:

Passing my driving test at the fourth attempt. If I hadn't passed after four tests, I was seriously thinking of getting someone else to do it for me. I couldn't stand the embarrassment any longer. My first instructor had a nervous breakdown, and the second one was incredibly fat and had a Mini, which meant he kept hitting the gear lever by mistake. He stank as well. Getting my Equity card was a wonderful moment as well.

COCK-UP:

I went to the wrong theatre for an audition – it turned out it had been closed for 25 years. It was being decorated at the time and one of the builders took pity on me and took me to the real theatre in his van. I was an hour and a half late and I've never forgotten it.

CARS:

My first was a Renault 5 which cost me £250 and broke down on the second day I had it. I have never had much luck with cars. Now I drive a Karmen Ghia.

HOME:

I've moved around a hell of a lot. My first place after leaving home was a bedsit in West Hampstead. It was a bit like *Rising Damp*, though the owner was an alcoholic 70-year-old woman who wore a matted blonde wig that was always the wrong way round. I lived on a houseboat on the Thames under the Hovis building. We had some great parties but it was freezing cold and damp and it was murder trying to get over the gangplank in stilettos. Now I live in a one-bedroom flat in S.W.10.

HOLIDAYS:

Greece is probably my favourite place – it's so romantic and beautiful. I went to Los Angeles on holiday recently and met the painter David Hockney, which was a memorable moment. I also spent a lot of time sunbathing by the pool which was wonderfully relaxing.

FOOD:

Caesar salad, garlic bread, Burger King veggie burgers and Weetabix – but not all at the same time.

DRINK:

Yes please! I love Margaritas, white wine and anything vodka-ish.

MUSIC:

Music has always been a very important part of my life. I have been in several bands over the years including Mari Wilson and The Wilsations! I was a Wilsation and had to have my hair in a beehive. I always like music around me.

BOOKS:

The Wasp Factory, *The Lost Weekend* and *Dream Dictionary*.

ADMIRE:

My mum – she will know why. And Anna Scher because she made it all possible for working-class kids to get into the business and to be thought of as actors, and not just stereotyped cockneys. Also, Ian McKellen for what he has done for the theatre and for being dangerous. Julie Walters, too, she's a great actress. I was in *Personal Services* with her and I was really in awe.

HEIGHT:

5ft 6in.

HOBBIES:

I hate that word because you always think of stamp collecting and things like that. I enjoy going to the cinema, shopping, going to the country for the weekend, travelling, having lots of friends around me. Anything so long as I don't have to sit at home and watch TV on my own or do housework.

FILM:

I like *Oliver* – I must have seen it six times and I still cry. *Alfie*'s brilliant too, also *Cat On A Hot Tin Roof*. *Mean Streets* is my favourite modern film. The music's brilliant.

AMBITION:

To make a great British film and to write a book.

FRIGHTENING MOMENT:

I cut half of my finger off when a friend of mine slammed a door on it. It was the one next to the little finger on my right hand. I fainted immediately, then I was in such absolute agony that I didn't realise what I had done until I looked down and saw the cut-off half on the floor. I picked it up and put it in a gravy bowl of ice until we got to hospital. They operated and gave me loads of stitches but I had to wait three days to see if it would work. I really thought I was going to lose my finger. I didn't.

FANCY:

Lots of people, though it normally doesn't last very long. I tend to go for interesting men as opposed to macho, bimbo men. They must have a sense of humour. I think Billy Connolly would be fun, Daniel Day-Lewis is gorgeous and Andy Garcia's quite cute too.

FIRST KISS:

In the playground of my junior school with Keith Harvey. I wonder what on earth happened to him. We were playing Dare, True Love, Kiss or Promise. I held his lips and kissed him and I couldn't look at him for a week afterwards. I was nine years old at the time.

FIRST BONK:

It was very disappointing – that's all I can say. I was 16 and it was in a bed, not somewhere sleazy like a park or a car. But it wasn't anything like as good as I had been led to believe. I think the guy concerned lasted about two days after that!

PAUL DANIELS

NAME:
Newton Edward Daniels. When I was a local government internal auditor, that name suited me fine. I was always called Ted then. But it didn't work out so well when I started doing magic on TV. My eldest son was called Paul and I thought, 'Yeah, that sounds good I'll use that.'

NICKNAME:
Sex Symbol, Superstud, the usual ones. I was called Shadrack at school – he was one of the guys in the lion's den and it seemed to fit me. It was a very intelligent school!

BORN:
4 April 1938. I was born in South Bank, off the Tees in North Yorkshire. My mum is Nancy, same as my brother and we are very worried about him. Father is Handel Newton Daniels, after the musician, scientist and religion. He gets called Huey.

SCHOOL:
My first school was Upper Prince's Street; I was the only boy in that school to pass an exam that took me into a grammar school. I was from a highly industrialised terraced road and didn't see a tree until I was 11. People shouldn't teach until they are 35 because otherwise they don't leave school, do they – ever? They don't get a real job, they need to come away from education and then go back and do it. I'd like to get involved in education. I got five O levels and then I wanted to get out.

JOBS:
My dad used to fix me up with jobs. He has been ace at everything he's done – he is the best mechanic, electrician, etc. – the most practical man I have ever known. He had a stroke 18 months ago and the week before he had dug a 100-yard trench through my woods to lay some pipes down. The day he had the stroke he'd been in a tractor bulldozing ground. He is

half-paralysed now but still tells gags and makes people laugh which is great. I considered becoming a woodwork teacher because I used the workshops to create illusions. I was offered the job of journalist, solicitor and others because my attitude was good; I was willing to learn if it interested me.

CAREER:

I wanted to be a professional magician from the age of 11. But society's view was that I should get a steady job, get married and procreate. I was 28 when my marriage started to break up. We really weren't getting along together, we got married because she was pregnant. It wasn't right. It was sad. Now I am married to Debbie which is the best thing I ever did in my life. But I think I will see a time in my life when there are a lot of old people who are very lonely because divorce has been the in thing. You have to stick in there, work at it. Now you give and give, and really try. I am 20 years older than Debbie and no argument is so important that I have got to lose the rest of my life.

COCK-UP:

The biggest cock-up was when I opened at the Savoy Theatre last year. On the first night, the finale number arrived and the computer jumped its lighting sequence so when the curtains went up there were all these halogen lights blazing. It looked ghastly. I said kill it and start again. And I explained to the audience that I wanted it to work properly and I ad-libbed until it was re-set. The second time, the lights changed perfectly and one of the three guys involved passed out. So we started again. I said, 'No, that's not supposed to happen either. But this is still my favourite illusion.' So I sat and chatted to the audience for about ten minutes. Then, when we got the green light, I walked up to the mike and said, 'This used to be my favourite illusion.'

GREATEST MOMENT:

I remember when my catchphrase 'I like it, Not A Lot, but I Like It' was put into the *Oxford Dictionary Of Slang*. I was blown away by that – I couldn't believe it. I developed it when I was being heckled by a guy in this working men's club called The Rainbow Rooms in Bradford. He said he didn't like my suit. I said, 'That's a shame because I like yours – not a lot, but I like it.' People laughed and there's an old comedic ploy that if you get a laugh you keep on using it. I applied that to the next trick. I said this is a good trick, you'll like this, not a lot, etc. and that got another laugh and I had my catchphrase.

HOME:

My first real home was Gifford's Barn, a stone-built home with a pool. I bought it ten days before Christmas and we were all sitting round and a load of Champagne arrived from Harrods. I thought, 'This is a bloody long way from Lower Oxford Street, South Bank.' Now I live in Roger Moore's old house, which is confusing for the locals because we look alike. I will never move unless I'm forced out. I am garden management, Debbie is garden labour – that's the way it should be!

CARS:

My first car was a 1938 8-horse power Standard wooden floors saloon, with drop-top cut-away doors and 16 coats of hand-rubbed cellulose. I bought it for £5 off a scrapheap and rebuilt it. It was my pride and joy, I split it red and black, with headlamps that stood up off the mudguards. Now I've got a Bentley 8, a Ferrari 308GTS, registration number MAG1C. And a Sinclair C5, because I was barred from the BBC car park one day by a bumptious attendant. The next day I bought the very first C5, which was the one on the news that night. I drove up to Wood Lane next time he was on duty and drove straight under the barrier – it was fantastic!

HOLIDAYS:

I love America. Japan is great outside Tokyo. But, for me, to go up and down the Nile on a cruise is extraordinary. Just amazing.

FOOD:

I like roast beef, Yorkshire pudding, and double egg and chips. I've had two great meals. The first was in a forest in Belgium. A qualified gourmet took me there – it was about 15 courses, each with different wine.

DRINK:

I don't drink a lot. I've never liked beer – I've got a very sweet tooth. I like Sancerre. But I usually drink Dubonnet with lemonade.

MUSIC:

I listen to Radio Four because I want plays, facts, quizzes. I don't really have a fixed musical taste. I'm astonished at the volume when I go to pop concerts.

BOOK:

My favourite book would be the *SAS Book Of Survival*.

HOBBIES:

Magic. I get paid for playing with my toys.

FILM:

The Wizard of Oz, *The Sting*, *Star Wars* because it was so innovative. *Jaws* because it was innovative directing.

ADMIRE:

I really admired Sammy Davis Jnr., who was the greatest entertainer of that kind we will ever see. Al Jolsen, too, was fantastic – and Michael Jackson's phenomenal. My favourite magician was Michael Brooke – the greatest magician of his time.

AMBITION:

I would like to be in a movie – in a cameo appearance, whatever. I love movies and I would like to be in one. There is no WOW in the British film industry – I'd put it there.

HATES:

People who drive in the centre lane of the motorways when the left lane is empty.

JIM DAVIDSON

FULL NAME:

James Cameron Davidson. I was supposed to be called Cameron James but my dad stopped off at the pub on the way to the Register office and, when he finally got there, he got them the wrong way round. Mum insisted on calling me Cameron and still does. It was a horrible name to grow up with so I stuck to Jim, much to her disappointment.

NICKNAME:

I was called Jock as a kid. Now it's The General – a name Jess Conrad gave me.

BORN:

13 December 1954 at my parents' home in Blackheath, South London. I'm a Sagittarius – I don't read my stars but people tell me I'm a typical example. My dad Jock died after 54 years of marriage to my mum Emmie. I've got two brothers, John and Billy, and two sisters, Eileen and Jean. I'm 10 years younger than any of them.

SCHOOL:

I loved school. They once banned us from letting off bangers in the playground so I let off an aerial bombshell and set fire to the woodwork shed – how dare they tell us what to do!

JOBS:

I did the lot – I was a window cleaner, messenger boy, clerk, van driver, porter, painter, forklift-truck driver, gardener, printer, air-ticket clerk, cashier and bacon boner. I was always being sacked because I could never get up on time. Now I'm always up by nine in the morning.

CAREER:

I didn't start my professional career until I was 20 – my first show was at the Black Bull pub in Lewisham – I had the Sunday lunch spot. Mum was great – she invented a completely bogus company called Astral Entertainments and would phone round all the restaurants and clubs to get me bookings. Then I got a break on *New Faces* and, at 24, I was the youngest comedian ever to appear at the London Palladium.

FRIGHTENING MOMENT:

When I was nine, I got shot in the eye by a catapult stone. I was taken to the Royal Eye Hospital because I was temporarily blinded. The tests I had done revealed I had tumours behind both eyes – talk about a lucky accident.

CAR:

I've had a Ferrari, Rolls-Royce and Escort XR3. I even had a Swedish four-ton commando truck. Now I've got a Bentley Turbo and a Range Rover.

HOLIDAYS:

My idea of bliss is taking my boat down to Torquay – it's a heavenly journey.

FOOD:

Curries are my favourite – but I'll eat anything really.

DRINK:

Light and bitter. I used to drink whisky a lot but it made

me fall over too much. My all-time favourite drink would be Remy Martin Louis XIII vintage brandy.

MUSIC:

I'm really into classical stuff at the moment – *The Tales Of Hoffman* is my favourite. I love the opera too. My favourite pop music would be from Keith Emerson, Pink Floyd and Yes.

BOOK:

The perfect way to relax is reading a good book. I enjoy reading about history – especially the First World War naval battles. I desperately wanted to be in the navy when I was younger and have an unlimited fascination for the subject. One of the best books I've read is *Soldier I*, the story of the SAS.

ADMIRE:

For me, the best comedian in Britain is Bernard Manning. He is totally filthy and has the capacity to offend just about every race and creed there is. But, underneath all that, a very warm and human personality shines through. You could fill an audience with people determined not to laugh at him, yet his professionalism would win through in the end. I did a show with him at the Palladium and all the other comedians on the bill were watching in the wings admiring his mastery. I admire Maggie Thatcher enormously too, and the Queen. And a wildlife painter called David Shepherd.

HEIGHT:
5ft 10in.

HOBBIES:
I used to be absolutely hooked on fishing – I was a member of Faversham Angling Club and the Carp Study Group and couldn't walk past a stretch of water without wanting to fish in it. But now I collect Japanese koi carp and I can't bear the thought of fishing any more. I've spent £50,000 on koi carp and a pond to put them in – and another £20,000 on a security system to protect them. I've got names for my favourites like Butterfly, Dopey and Bert. I want to enter them in competitions soon. I like racing too – I've got three horses and two greyhounds.

HATES:
Swimming – I'm ashamed of my skinny legs. And telephones – I don't answer them. I also hate people who can't be bothered, not being able to sleep at night and when I drink too much. I don't like a lot of people – Jimmy Savile claims he's his own worst enemy but he isn't while I'm around.

FILM:

Any of the *Carry On* films – they were all a great influence to me and I love them.

AMBITION:

To get the phone number of a certain waitress I met in a West End restaurant one day...

FRIGHTENING EXPERIENCE:

Heights – they are my greatest fear. I cannot stand being high up and looking down. Also when Mum collapsed on the way to my after-show party at Wimbledon Theatre. My driver John Baker, who used to work for Madonna, saw her go, leaped off stage, breaking his ankle at the same time, limped his way over and cleared everyone away. He did everything to revive her until the ambulance arrived. Mum had already had two heart attacks before this so we got her fitted with a pacemaker and she's been fine ever since. I'd say she was one in a million, she'd say I was won in a raffle.

FANCY:

My gorgeous wife Tracy.

BOBBY DAVRO

NAME:
Robert Nankeville. My father needed a name for his business so he took DAV from my brother David's name and RO from Robert, my first name. I liked the name so much I took it as a stage name.

NICKNAME:
Bobs is the only thing I get called, I suppose.

BORN:
13 September 1958. Ashford, Middlesex. Janet and Bill are my mum and dad's names. I have a sister called Janine and a brother called David. My dad's an Arfur Daley type – but he's retired now.

SCHOOL:

My first school was Staines Prep School. I lived just round the corner from there. Then I went to Hounslow College. I got English, maths and history O levels. I was always in with the boys who did the fighting, never the victim. I talked my way out of trouble. First day I got to Hounslow College, it looked like Baghdad library – all falling down. One poor lad got a slate on the head and it cut him badly. I was standing next to him. I was lazy – I gave up study for women at 15. I used to go out at lunchtime and see to an older woman in a clothes shop in the High Street. My dad was an Olympic athlete – he ran with Chataway, Bannister and Gordon Perry in the relay team. But I hated athletics. I used to get letters from my parents saying I was taking up golf so I could skip athletics. My brother was a pro and I got down to seven handicap. I play off 13 now but I'm really an eight or nine. Golf's a great game.

JOBS:

I was a lifeguard in a carwash for a while! And I worked at Bentalls, in Kingston, in the men's department doing my John Inman impressions. Then I worked for my dad and caused chaos. I was always dropping stuff.

CAREER:

I used to impersonate the teachers and take off Mike Yarwood's impressions. Then I saw him on a chat show saying how he was peeved that everyone used to copy his impressions so I started my own style. My real break was when I did *Live At Her Majesty's* with Jimmy Tarbuck in 1984. I did Elton John at the piano and stuff like that and it went down really well. I got my *Go For It* series out of that. But there are too many restrictions on TV for my liking – I can't be as risque as I would like to be. I haven't enjoyed the series this time round – I think it's time to move on really. I need some new stimulation. I don't think I will do another sketch show – I like working live. Perhaps a game show or something. I'd like to do the stuff I have never been able to do – because I've always been on early on Saturday nights. It's very frustrating. I don't always want to be the guy with funny voices.

FRIGHTENING MOMENT:

Doing the *Royal Command Show* three years ago. That's when I discovered that adrenalin was brown and runny. It was terrifying. It was a very scary show to do. I remember doing a sketch as Jim Bowen and I cocked it all up. I've still got a photo of me as him that day looking like death warmed up – sheer terror.

GREATEST MOMENT:
Live at Her Majesty's was great – the day I realised I had cracked it.

COCK-UP:
I think the worst I ever went down was at the Blackpool Opera House in front of 3,000 Rotarians. I bombed, no one laughed and I died a total death. Horrendous. It went down like Bobby Crush on an oil rig. The one thing that develops comedy is when you die. I still get nights like that. I played an audience of Japanese people and they didn't understand a bloody thing.

CARS:
The first one was an Austin 1100. I paid a monkey for it. Now I drive a Toyota Celica Turbo, 4-wheel drive. I've always liked Toyotas. And I've got a Mercedes for all the heavy motorway work.

HOME:
I live in Staines, Middlesex.

HOLIDAYS:
I had a wonderful time in Cyprus, and a great American tour round New York, Las Vegas and Disneyworld.

FOOD:

I like curries but I put on so much weight when I eat them.

DRINK:

I like wine, but not beer really, though the odd pint's nice. A nice white Chablis is good with salad.

MUSIC:

I have a lot of records – Elton John's brilliant. My first record was 'Sugar Sugar' by the Archies. My favourite though was Gilbert O'Sullivan, he was fantastic.

BOOK:

I like Stephen King – he wrote a great book called *It*.

ADMIRE:

I admire Robin Williams enormously. He's superb with those quick-fire lines. And Billy Connolly is wonderful as well.

FILM:

Raiders of the Lost Ark was good. I like lovey-dovey ones too. I'd love to see *Love Story* – I've never seen it. I like *Star Wars*, anything that can stretch the imagination. It has to take me away from everyday business.

AMBITION:

To make a film, eventually, or maybe make a record. I do a lot of singing.

FANCY:

Michelle Pfeiffer. Shirley MacLaine always fascinated me, I loved her. I also like Kim Basinger, I wouldn't kick her out of bed anyway.

FIRST KISS:

I was about eight. She was a girl called Stephanie Grimshaw. I was very young so it was like a quick peck. Then Susan Lucas came along when I was 12 and that was a proper smacker.

FIRST BONK:

It frightened me because I was on my own. No, seriously, I lost my virginity to a girl in a holiday camp. I was 15, she was two years older and it was very, very clumsy.

LES DENNIS

NAME:
My real name is Leslie Heseltine, no relation. A few years ago, I rented a house from this very posh lady called Lady Benn. When she greeted me, she added pompously, 'No relation of course.' It was great to be able to reply, 'Me neither.'

NICKNAME:
I was called Lightbulb at school because I was so blond. I loathed my hair colour because of all the teasing.

BORN:
Liverpool in 1953. Dad was Leslie, Mum Winnifred

Grimes. I've got a brother Ken, and two sisters Amanda and Margaret.

SCHOOL:

I followed The Beatles around a bit. My first school was Stockton Wood Primary, where Paul McCartney went, then to Joseph Williams where Paul also went, then Quarry Bank where Lennon formed the Quarrymen. I always looked for a desk with Lennon's name on but never found anything. I stayed on to do A levels because I was in the drama group and wanted to be in the play. I looked through my report the other day and it said I was good when I was there – 49 days' absence in my last term! Clive Barker, the horror writer, was in my class and took over the drama class. And Steve Coppell was in the football team so I never got into that either. I remember in the second form at Quarry when this mate of mine Peter Fright asked if I wanted a fight at 4 p.m. He said all the other guys had told him he couldn't beat me. I thought about this and said OK, and we had a right old scrap behind the bike sheds until the headmaster broke it up. It was a draw.

CAREER:

I played at working men's clubs from the age of 17. I was on *Opportunity Knocks* at 17 and came fourth. A

Scots singer called Stuart Gillies won – he lives in Jersey now. His hit was called 'Amanda'.

PAINFUL EXPERIENCE:
I took a bad beating from some football thugs. I had been to the pub with some mates in Manchester and we fancied some fish and chips. A gang of Sunderland supporters spotted us and gave chase. I was the only one they caught. They punched me to the ground and started kicking me in the head and ribs. I was terrified and thought I'd had it. I was bleeding from the head and covered in bruises and cuts. Then I put on a Geordie accent and told them I wasn't a Manchester United supporter. Finally, they believed me and stopped. They even apologised and helped me to my feet. My accent saved me really – I hate to think what would have happened otherwise. I haven't been to a soccer match since.

GREATEST MOMENT:
Playing in a charity football match at Anfield in 1984. There was quite a crowd and I scored a goal at the Kop end, where I had stood for years. Derek Hatton passed it from the left wing and I put it in the back of the net – a massive cheer went up and it was a brilliant moment. On a personal level, the birth of my son Phillip was wonderful.

COCK-UP:

I was in panto with Dustin Gee and we were playing two village idiots in bright costumes. It was a quick costume change scene and I put on these clothes and thought they were a bit big. It turned out we'd put on each other's costume. I looked baggy but his costume looked terrible. He was not amused.

CARS:

An Austin Maxi was my first, the number plate was TUN 194J. I had a better car than some of the teachers at school because I was doing quite well then. Now I have a BMW 325i convertible.

HOME:

Archway, North London, right on the railway line. It's a converted old workshop. Very yuppy, I know.

HOLIDAYS:

I like villa holidays by the pool.

FOOD:

Good pasta and Chinese, a choice between the two usually.

DRINK:

Australian red wines are my tipple at the moment.

MUSIC:
Tom Waites, Aztec Camera, Elvis Costello, Elton John, Creedence Clearwater Revival. My favourite album would be Elton's *Captain Fantastic* or Tom Waits's *The Asylum Years*.

BOOK:
John Irving's *The World According To Garp*.

ADMIRE:
Ken Dodd for his sheer professionalism and enthusiasm and for being so funny. Woody Allen's tremendous too.

HEIGHT:
5ft 9in. People think I am smaller on TV than I am. But that's because I work with big guys like Russ Abbot.

HOBBIES:
I like going to good plays. I play golf badly. I used to run a lot and want to get back into it. But I'm still recovering from a hernia operation so it's tricky.

FILM:
It would be have to be the unedited version of *The Godfather*.

AMBITION:
I would like to do a stage play in the West End. There have been some sketch characters I've done I would like to expand.

HATES:
Outside lane drivers on the motorway who won't move over and pretentious people who won't be themselves.

FRIGHTENING MOMENT:
My agent, Roger, and me were walking back from this restaurant in Richmond, West London and this guy came up for what I thought was an autograph. But, when I turned round, I saw he had blood all over his knuckles. He looked totally mad – it was like a horror film. I shouted at Roger to run and we legged it, with this lunatic chasing after us. I jumped over a hedge and got away. But then I thought, 'Sod this I'm not running away from this bloke.' So I grabbed my credit cards, went back to him and stupidly said, 'Police!' That prompted him to chase after me again. He got within feet of us when Roger picked up a fence stake and threatened him with it. That seemed to scare him off. I eventually got home and locked the door. We laughed about it later but it was bloody frightening at the time.

FANCY:

Thora Hird, she's great. No, seriously, Melanie Griffiths. I was in Tramp once and I was out of my head. I went up to her and said, 'Melanie, I think you are brilliant.' She asked me who I was, so I slurred, 'My name's Les, do you wanna dance?' She very politely explained that she had a date already, and I looked round to see Michael Douglas. But she looked gorgeous, like Marilyn Monroe. Julia Roberts isn't bad either, is she?

FIRST KISS:

I remember taking a girl to the cinema and not kissing her. The next night, she and her mate took the piss out of me, which made me feel terrible. They reckoned I was a wimp. But I did get to kiss her later. I was 15 at the time – a bit naïve and a very late starter.

FIRST BONK:

I actually first did it on my wedding night. I know it sounds terribly corny. I was 19 and had never done it before and I didn't do it properly then! It may sound boring I know – but it's true.

NOEL EDMONDS

FULL NAME:
Noel Edmonds, but I am not telling you my middle names under any circumstances.

NICKNAME:
I was Eddie at school and I missed being called Randy West throughout my career by about 20 minutes. When I started on Radio Luxembourg, they wanted to call me that and I was in a weak position to argue because they were prepared to take me from school and make me a DJ. But, fortunately, the producer was late back from lunch and the others said, 'Sod it – keep your own name.' I hate to think what would have happened otherwise.

BORN:

22 December 1948 in Ilford, Essex. I vary between Capricorn and Sagittarius – but I'm not into all that stuff. My dad is a former headmaster called Dudley and Mum's an art teacher, Lydia. I am an only child.

SCHOOL:

My first school was Glade Primary, Ilford. I then went to a minor public school, Brentwood in Essex. Griff Rhys-Jones went there and Hardy Amies. I remember the total depression of being high up at primary school then going to a school where I didn't know French and Latin. It was not a happy time for me.

JOBS:

I worked in a toyshop in Romford at Christmas. Then I bought and sold go-karts and did gardening for various people – I was good at straight lines and neat edges for the lawn.

CAREER:

I used to make tapes at home pretending I was a DJ. I sent one off to Kenny Everett, who passed it to Ed Stewart. And I started hearing some of my gags on the air so I knew they had it. Then Tony Windsor, who ran Radio Luxembourg, phoned me up out of the blue and offered me a job. I read the news at first.

Luxembourg was good fun because they were reacting in 1969 to Radio One so everything was young and trendy. I was 19, Dave Jensen was 19, Paul Burnett, 23. We had a great laugh. It was my university. Then I moved on to peddle the biggest load of crap on Radio One's breakfast show. Amazingly, people do remember it fondly. I became part of people's lives – now those listeners ask me to sign autographs for their daughters!

COCK-UP:

My biggest cock-up was at Live Aid in 1985. I'd been working for three days sorting out the helicopter airlift. On the day, Bob Geldof and Harvey Goldsmith were giving me, like everyone else, a lot of pressure. I flew in Phil Collins and Bob told me to fucking introduce him myself. So I went out there and gave him a massive build-up before introducing Mr Phil Collins! And then Sting walked out... 100,000 people and billions of TV viewers saw me cringe. I walked off and wished I wasn't flying later because I wanted to get drunk.

CARS:

When I was 17, I bought an ex-European Airways Minivan from a man in Collindale and, should he ever read this, I want a word, because the gearbox packed up. I've gone off cars now because there are too many of them. I've got a Bentley Turbo, which is a super car, and perfect for all the motorway driving I do. It handles so beautifully.

HOME:

I live in a village called Broomford in Devon. I wanted somewhere nice for the kids to grow up. I enjoy farming and we've got a big place here now. It's a very useful antidote to the pressures of being in the public eye. It's private but not remote. I can get back from Wembley in three hours, which is easy. I hate London now and would never live there again.

HOLIDAYS:

Kids change everything. I used to pop off to a beach in Mauritius or the Seychelles. But probably the best place now is Disneyworld. They looked after us so well there.

FOOD:

I am a philistine really, I'm happy with a Big Mac. I like Chinese, and hate nouvelle cuisine. I admire the French style of cooking – but I don't get passionate about it.

DRINK:

I am very fond of Dom Perignon Champagne. A bottle of that and a beautiful woman and I'm happy.

MUSIC:

I like the Eurythmics, Phil Collins, Def Leppard, Vivaldi, a bit of Mozart. Bruce Springsteen's great for the beach. My first record was Elvis's 'Fool Such As I' and 'That Certain Smile' by Johnny Mathis. He was quite a swinger at the time! My favourite album would be anything from Springsteen.

BOOK:

Wind In The Willows – I loved it as a kid. And Jeremy Lloyd's *Captain Beaky* stuff was wonderful. But I generally prefer magazines to books.

ADMIRE:

I admire David Attenborough enormously. It's very difficult to make part of TV your own but he does it in an entertaining way, but he is also a little odd – he's a strong character with his own mannerisms. Alan Whicker's the same. And Rowan Atkinson – I boggle at that man's talent.

HEIGHT:

5ft 7in.

HOBBIES:

I'm keen on photography, and video for the family. I like gardening and forestry. But I love flying most – the discipline and freedom.

FILM:

Vanishing Point.

AMBITION:

I am very ambitious, always have been. Life is a series of opportunities. It annoys me when I see talented people who have missed their chance.

FRIGHTENING MOMENT:

I had a helicopter catch fire when I was flying it. It did concentrate my thought pattern for a while. But my most terrifying moment was when I hosted the *Royal Variety Show*. I stood in the wings and saw the Queen come in and take her seat and I was shaking like a leaf. I couldn't move, I couldn't remember my lines, and I was rigid. I got it together just in time but I've never had nerves like that. I left the stage dripping in sweat. It's a hell of an opportunity to drop a major bollock.

FANCY:

I fancy one other woman and that is Ginny Leng, the horsewoman. She has a great behind and very pretty face. My wife lets me fancy her because she admires what she has done in her career. And I do fancy my wife like mad – we've been married for five years but I still look at her and think, 'Cor!'

FIRST KISS:
I remember sitting next to a girl I will call Mary on the bus to the swimming baths when I was eight. She was my first love. I met her again recently and it was very embarrassing. She was NOT how I remembered her at all – which is the politest way of putting it. She is now extremely unattractive! It felt horrible – doesn't everyone find that?

HARRY ENFIELD

FULL NAME:
Henry Richard Enfield.

NICKNAME:
Harry.

BORN:
30 May 1961 at Horsham Hospital, Horsham. My parents live in Billingshurst, West Sussex. I've got a sister Sue, who lives in Africa with her husband, and two younger sisters Lucy and Lizzie. My mum, Deirdre, is a secretary at Sotheby's auction rooms. My dad, Edward, is a director with West Sussex County Council. We are a close family now, though

we didn't use to be because we kids all went to different schools.

SCHOOL:

I was at Worth public school for two years. It was a horrible elitist place run by monks who called themselves Christian but were the epitome of everything that's not at all Christian. I was a punk when I did my A levels. I didn't do any work, dyed my hair black and cut it really short. I was a carrier-bag punk – I'd leave home in flares and change into my painted trousers up the road. Being a punk meant skipping classes and going to 50p gigs in Camden. And, if you could play three chords on a guitar, you were in a band. We used to fight the government – whichever party was in at the time. It makes me laugh to see how establishment I've become. I was quite small and fat at school and used to hang around with the tough guys which meant you had to develop an acerbic nastiness towards other boys so you could make the tough guys laugh. I scraped into York University. I missed out on the social life at York because I was playing at being a husband with my then girlfriend. My parents were upset because they thought I was too young. They were proved right of course.

CAREER:

I formed my first comedy act with a mate called Bryan Elsley – we were spotted by the BBC at the Edinburgh Festival. Then John Lloyd hired me to do Jimmy Greaves, David Steel and Douglas Hurd's voices for *Spitting Image* after seeing me at the Crown and Castle in Dalston, East London. I got £176 for a Saturday shift. My big break came when I did a mimic of Prince Philip visiting his local kebab shop, where his cousin worked. An editor of *Saturday Night Live* was watching and Stavros was born.

FEARS:

I find stage shows very nerve-wracking. I pace up and down beforehand, smoking and drinking lots of Coca-Cola. Standing there on your own trying to make people laugh is scary. For me, it's a bit like going to see the headmaster.

EMBARRASSING MOMENT:

I had to walk down Oxford Street half-naked when we did the TV fashion show *Frocks On The Box* which I co-presented with Marie Helvin and Muriel Gray. I think they set out to deliberately humiliate me and it worked – I was looking for an autumn outfit. They got me into schoolboy outfits. I only agreed to do the show when I was drunk one night

– oh no, I didn't mean that, it was the highlight of my career.

CARS:

I've never been into flash cars. That goes back to my parents who had things like 17-year-old Hillman Hunters – they got cross with people who thought they were good because of what they had rather than who they were. I used to drive a D-reg Vauxhall Cavalier but it got such a pain in the neck driving around London that I sold it and bought a bicycle. It's great – I am a lot fitter and I get everywhere quicker. I had five cars in 1987, things kept happening to them. One blew up in a gas explosion, and another was stolen. But I'm useless with them – I can't change a wheel or find the oil dipstick. If something goes wrong, I'm depressed for days.

I also used to have a great scam going. A traffic warden I knew gave me a sign I could put in the back of the car, which had three initials that would tell the authorities I could park anywhere because I was a traffic warden. But they rumbled me eventually and towed me away. They threatened to accuse me of impersonating a traffic warden.

HOME:

I live in a two-bedroom flat in Primrose Hill, North

London. The mortgage is exactly £100,000 and I, like everyone else, have trouble paying it every month.

HOLIDAYS:
Anywhere hot and interesting – I used to pack a bag on my back and go off for months on end, it was great fun.

FOOD:
I love food – I'll eat Indian, Chinese, Greek, Italian, French, British, Indonesian, in fact anything except beetroot and raw fish. I used to like nothing better than being invited to great big feeds but now I watch my diet a little better. I'm a useless cook though so I tend to eat out with friends in North London.

DRINK:
I used to drink a lot of lager and whisky but I've cut down recently. You can't work flat out and booze every night, it makes you feel terrible. But I'm still hopelessly addicted to coffee and cigarettes.

MUSIC:
I like the opera, Frank Sinatra, Elvis Costello and Rachmaninoff.

BOOK:
I read a lot – anything that's around really.

ADMIRE:

Alexei Sayle. David Jason – I think *Only Fools and Horses* is the best sitcom there has been for years. And Rik Mayall is the funniest man I know. He can go on stage, be thoroughly nasty and everyone laughs. That's genius. Rik can say 'What!' for ten minutes and people will die laughing. He's got tremendous cheek and I admire and envy his presence. Of the older generation, I thought Terry Thomas and Kenneth Williams were wonderful. Ben Elton told me Terry Thomas had died and he was almost crying. Ben's great, he's the only good political comedian to emerge in the last 20 years.

HEIGHT:

5ft 10in.

HOBBIES:

I like walking round Highgate Cemetery – I get a lot of inspiration sitting next to Karl Marx's grave. It's just round the corner from my house. I love duck watching as well – I picked York University because they had a lot of ducks.

AMBITION:

I would like to make a documentary on Gerard Hoffnung. He was a brilliant Hungarian cartoonist who died in 1958, three years before I was born. But a mate of mine had a record of his and I think he's a genuinely witty man. And never crude. I love his painting too. He was an eccentric guy – apparently, his ambition was to put on a Berlioz symphony played on a hill in Dorking by an orchestra of 2,000 wearing binoculars.

HATES:

I despise all politicians – they are all liars and fools. The whole country hates them, which is why political satire is so popular. I don't support any party in particular, though I lean towards the Labour Party, I suppose. But I hate pint-of-beer socialism. There is nothing wrong in having a car that works – you don't have to wear sackcloth and ashes to be a socialist. I also hate forgetting people's names when I am introduced to them.

FRIGHTENING MOMENT:

I was heckled off stage at the Albert Hall. There were 5,000 people there for a benefit for the Colombian disaster. I'd been going really well for ten minutes when I thought I'd do Stavros. But they all thought I was taking the piss out of South Americans. It was a bad move. What made it worse was they had just announced Pete Townshend would be on in a minute. They booed me off. I like heckling from the

Loadsamoney fans – so long as they shut up eventually and let me get on with the show. If I see couples sitting there in Pringle sweaters, I think, 'Good.' But it's the *Guardian* readers in their leather jackets, glasses and stripy shirts that I hate. They come to see this interesting phenomenon and ask themselves if Loads is overstepping the boundaries of satire. The simple answer is, of course, that he is a loud, bleedin' git. I remember one drunken woman in her forties jumping up once and asking me what I thought about the plight of the Indians in Peru. What do you say? I just told her to f*** off, though I felt bad about it later.

FIRST BONK:

It took me a long time to lose my virginity. I was desperate to do it on my 16th birthday and went to all the girls at the party saying, 'Do you want to snog and do you want to do it?' But I was too fat and stupid and nobody liked me. When it finally happened, I can hardly remember it. I have blotted it completely from my memory because it wasn't a pleasant experience. She said, 'Is that it?' and all I could say was: 'I'm afraid it is.'

KENNY EVERETT
1943-1995

FULL NAME:
Maurice Cole.

NICKNAME:
My mum, sister and father call me Mo, short for Maurice.

BORN:
In the front room of our house in Hereford Road, Liverpool. Dad's name was Tom and Mum's Lil. My sister is Kate.

SCHOOL:
St Thomas' School, then St Edmonds middle school

and St Jude's secondary modern. My most vivid memory is being belted by the headmaster across the backs of my calves with a strap for being late. I hated school so I was always late. My reports always said, 'Kenny tries when he wants to' – which wasn't very often. I failed my 11 plus – I had a DJ brain.

JOBS:

I scraped gunge off sausage-roll tins, then I went into an advertising agency called Douglas and Co in Liverpool. I fired myself after four years because they were about to put me in charge of the place while the manager went on holiday. To save us going bust while I was the boss, I resigned!

CAREER:

I made a tape of me doing a show for my chums and sent it to the BBC. I liked the whole atmosphere of the BBC – they had carpets which went to the walls instead of just the middle of the room. And everyone called each other darling, which made me think it was perfect for me. I asked for a job but they suggested I try a pirate station called Radio London – the Big L. That was in 1965. My big break came when Ringo Starr grabbed a jelly baby on stage and ate it when The Beatles were absolutely huge. Within days, every concert hall they played was full of flying jelly babies.

Bassetts, the company who made them, asked my station if they had a Liverpudlian DJ who would follow The Beatles around America for them and report back on a nightly show. So I went on an all-expenses round trip and spent months with them. They were rough and wacky and jolly and wrote good tunes. They were much more sophisticated than me, though, it was like talking to a double set of Morecambe and Wise. I found them overawing until I realised they were human. I've never been good at interviewing and I remember asking John Lennon a stupid question and he leaned over and said in a thick Liverpool accent, 'You're not very good, are you, Ken?' I died on the spot. Paul heard that, took me into the bathroom and told me to ask him anything and he would rattle on long enough for me to have five days' worth of show! I said, 'How are you?' and he very kindly gave me a load of great stories and anecdotes. He was kind to a struggling idiot and I have appreciated that ever since.

COCK-UP:

I joined Radio One when it first started, and they gave me my own show after six months. They were like a bunch of schoolmasters in charge of what they regarded as idiots, and kept us on a tight leash. I did a two-hour show and it was very complicated. They got me to operate my own equipment, which was very old and not easy to work. I kept on at the controller, this very grand, white-haired old boy, to change the studio. One day, he did the lot – updated the whole thing. I turned up five minutes before the show and had no idea what to do. It was a total fuck-up from start to finish, every single song went appallingly wrong and I was desperate. Just when it reached its bloodiest moment, I looked up and saw this old man smiling as if to say, 'You wanted it, now you've got it.' I got fired eventually for a comment I made after a news item about the Minister of Transport's wife passing her driving test.

CARS:
My first was a washing machine on wheels called a Fiat 125. I remember driving it out of the showroom very proudly – and straight into an E-Type Jaguar. But the E-Type was driven by an Arab, who must have either forgotten to apply for his road tax or had a load of drugs stuffed in the back because he ranted and raved for ten minutes then drove off! Now I have a BMW.

HOME:
I live in Kensington, West London. I shall move off to the country in three years when I retire. I am quitting to write books about travel and things.

I'll be 50 and I've got to enjoy the huge pension I've amassed.

HOLIDAYS:
I remember drinking in a bar at Hawaii Airport and not hearing any announcement. I remember thinking it was rather odd – then I went outside just in time to see my Jumbo taking off. It turned out they didn't have any announcements there. I like America and Australia, where my parents and sister live. Russia was interesting. I would like to go to Rio one day for the carnival – and dance myself to death.

FOOD:
I like English, Indian, anything really.

HATES:
Getting up in the morning. I have such wonderful dreams that waking up is such an anti-climax.

FILM:
It's a Wonderful Life with James Stewart. Very weepy black and white thing they wheel out at Christmas. *When Harry Met Sally* made me laugh a lot too.

DRINK:
I used to drink a bottle of brandy a day in early 80s

but I just pulled out of the slide in time to save my liver. Now I drink about two glasses of whisky a day.

AMBITION:

To travel more – do Europe very slowly, perhaps on foot. I'd like to amble through France eating cheap baguettes and swigging cheap wine.

MUSIC:

Brahms is my favourite, and Mozart is rather jolly too. I like a lot of rock music too. The only thing I don't like is reggae. It's too repetitive. My first single was 'Wake Up Little Susie' by The Everly Brothers. My favourite singer would be Paul Simon, I think.

FIRST KISS:

It was a woman who used to be a friend of my mother's who had a brown moustache and smoked a lot of cigarettes without the tips. She used to say, 'Oh, Mo, my favourite,' then throw herself towards me and kiss me like a sink plunger. I gave it another try later and it was a lot better.

BOOK:

A paperback I stumbled across called *The Long Walk* by Slavimir Rawicz. It was about how he escaped from a concentration camp in Siberia to India and it's the only book that has ever made me cry. A very sad and moving book.

ADMIRE:
Steve Martin is my favourite comedian by a hundred million miles – he's the only man in the world I would rather be than myself.

HEIGHT:
5ft 6in.

HOBBIES:
Travelling.

FIRST BONK:
Not a chance... When I was revealed to be gay, I was walking along the road and this scaffold worker saw me below, took his trousers down, waved his willy about and said, 'How about this, Kenny?' I shouted back to him, 'Oh yes,' and he had to fold it back in, very embarrassed.

KEITH FLOYD

FULL NAME:
Keith Floyd.

NICKNAME:
They used to call me Bomber in the army, but I don't
know why.

BORN:
28 December 1943 in Reading, Berkshire. Mum was
Gwyn, Dad was Syd. I have a sister called Brenda.

SCHOOL:
My first was Wiveliscombe Primary School. I was
quite bright but not very well behaved. I seemed to be

permanently in trouble. I fought a lot and usually came out OK, on top at least! I never did any cooking at school at all. But I was always a country lad so I'd go out fishing and catching trout and cooking them. That interest developed into a job. The first thing I ever cooked was when I was 12. I was staying at a friend's farm and I cooked roast beef with potatoes and cabbage – the works. It went down very well.

JOBS:

I worked on a farm in the long holidays, swept the pavement at a paper shop and bottled up in the local pub.

CAREER:

I never did a cookery course. I went along to a big hotel in Bristol when I was 22 and said to the manager I was very serious but had no qualifications. My first job was to cook a vat of beetroots, but I watched everyone else and asked lots of questions, before moving on. I did that many times over two years and it served as a good apprenticeship. I think Elizabeth David has been my biggest influence. She wrote a series of wonderful books about French cooking which were so authentic and unfussy. She made me want to go to the place where the dish originated. She was a very beguiling writer. The quality of writing attracted me.

GREATEST MOMENT:

I was very thrilled when I read that Prince Philip watches all my videos regularly. And I was watching the *Aspel* show when Norman Tebbit was asked how he coped with the cooking, now his wife was disabled, and he replied that he just watched Floyd and copied him. That sort of thing is really great.

COCK-UP:

Dozens. The best one was my first ever TV programme. I cooked a wonderful guinea fowl with peaches in a brandy-flavoured sauce. I got to the point that all I had to do under the cameras was cut it up and serve it. I cut through the middle only to find the little plastic bag of giblets was still there, untouched.

CARS:

The first was a 1935 yellow Austin 7, which I paid £5 for. Now I drive a Bentley and an XJS Jaguar. I bought the Bentley on an impulse – I was passing the showroom and I thought, 'Why not?'

HOLIDAYS:

I like working holidays. I have a small place in Southern Ireland where I go and fish, garden, watch rugby and have a few pints of Murphy's.

FOOD:

A roast leg of lamb, with new potatoes lifted straight from the plot, plus some fresh broad beans and runner beans – that would be my all-time favourite meal. For dessert, a bowl of raspberries with real Devon clotted cream. My object when serving customers is to please. If I agree with a customer who complains, then I will replace their meal immediately. If they then start going over the top, I tell them to fuck off. If they want to get shitty, they get it back in spades.

HOME:

My place is called the Maltsters Arms, in a village called Tuckenhay, South Devon.

DRINK:

Murphy's stout, Scotch whisky and all the red wines from the Rhone valley. I've been pissed on TV – but then so has everyone else. I remember doing a chat show in Australia and I had too much Champagne and got fairly wibbly-wobbly. They gave me some coffee before I went on, but all that made me do was go on stage and say, 'This coffee is crap' before pouring it over the floor. The audience absolutely loved it. The TV station have invited me back – I hope they are not disappointed when I turn up sober.

MUSIC:
I love Bob Dylan.

BOOK:
Mervyn Peake's book *Titus Alone*.

HEIGHT:
6ft 2in.

HOBBIES:
Fishing, reading and listening to music.

FILM:
Casablanca, though it changes all the time.

AMBITION:
People say I am extremely ambitious, but I don't think
I am. I just want to carry on doing a fairly decent job
and not be under pressure all the time.

HATES:
I don't like all sorts of things – hippies, they're out of
date and should change into something more
modern. Bad manners I loathe.

FANCY:
Nearly every woman I see. The Features Editor of

Today is very nice looking and Kim Basinger's lovely too. Women do send me quite extraordinary mail sometimes. One faxed a nude photograph of herself together with a rather explicit menu for romance, which I declined.

FIRST KISS:

A most embarrassing experience. I was about 13 and it was one of those silly situations on the school bus where we passed notes to the girls on the bus asking to meet them later. Her name was Susan and I didn't know how to do it.

FIRST BONK:

It put me off for a while. I was quite old by today's standards, about 20 I think.

GARETH HALE

FULL NAME:
Gareth Irving Hale. (I don't try to keep the middle name a secret.)

NICKNAME:
That fat git! Gal, Gaz, anything short and easy. But not Giant Haystack or Flutterbuttock – which Norman calls me after a few certain meals.

BORN:
15 January 1953 in Brixton, London.

SCHOOL:
I went to Hollymount Infants and Junior School in

Raynes Park, South London. I was an average kid, just happy to be there. I was good at English, I enjoyed creative writing. But my vivid imagination used to get me into trouble. My worst day came when my teacher asked me to write a little poem and I tried to hide mine and I was made to read it out – and I got slippered. It went something like: 'My dog is a naughty thing, so I kick his balls and make them ring!' I was eight, so my career started then! In fact, we used that rhyme in the last series. Sport was always my favourite subject – especially rugby, which I still love. It seemed natural to go on to PE college – which is where I met Norm.

JOB:
I did a Sunday-morning paper round which paid double bubble – ten bob, which was bloody good.

CAREER:
In the sixth form at school, I did my first show with selected parts from *Under Milk Wood*. Then I met Norman and we used to go down to the college folk clubs and try to outdo the other comedians. The Tramshed was our big break – we played there every week for seven years. We would write a new act every fortnight and learn it, which was a brilliant apprenticeship. Then we got offered a pilot for Radio Four. It was outrageous, one of the Governors of the

BBC actually wrote to our producer David Hatch and said this stuff was so disgusting we should be thrown off, but we survived.

FRIGHTENING MOMENT:

Waiting to go on at the *Royal Variety Show* in 1987. It was terrifying. You sit there waiting to go on with people like Shirley Bassey and Tom Jones and you think, 'GOD.' Personally, being with my wife before our first baby Shan was born was scary too, It was much more of a pleasure second time around.

GREATEST MOMENT:

Watching my daughter Shan being born, particularly because both my other daughters were born when we were on tour. We were in York on the date she was due and I didn't think I'd get back in time but it just so happened I managed to get back that day and I was there for the whole thing, all night. Seeing that little head coming out was such a shaking moment. I knew then I would bore the arse off hundreds of people for the rest of my life telling them about it.

COCK-UP:

During filming of the last series, there was a sketch called *The Man Who Couldn't Take Anything Seriously*. He has a series of horrible things happen to him, like being fired from work, but he can't stop laughing. There was one scene where he was sitting at a riverbank with his wife and she told him she'd been unfaithful and he kept laughing. This girl who was with me cocked up her lines, so I tried to relax her by telling her to have a good old breathe in and out. And to make her laugh I added, 'Just think, if you get through this, you can bury that horrible dress they've you to wear.' She said she given couldn't do that because it was HER dress. The soundman heard every word and fell off his chair laughing. But I felt awful. I was cringing.

CARS:
First one was a Renault 4, which was green underneath all the bird shit. Now I've got a BMW 735i.

HOLIDAYS:
The best ever was a holiday in Jamaica with some mates – it was brilliant.

FOOD:
Indian, I love curries and lager. I like them not too strong with coconut flavouring.

DRINK:
Tequila and orange juice or margarita – but only when I can't drink any more lager...

MUSIC:
I like Erasure. The first record I bought was by The Beatles – but I can't remember which one.

BOOK:
The Ginger Man by J. P. Donleavy. It's about a wild and crazy Irish bloke – a bit like Frank Carson.

ADMIRE:
I enjoy watching Steve Martin and John Cleese.

HEIGHT:
5ft 8in.

HOBBIES:
Travelling, I like seeing new countries and meeting new people.

FAVOURITE FILM:
On The Waterfront.

AMBITION:
To make a film with someone like Robin Williams and Steve Martin.

HATES:
I hate people who queue-barge – it always happens

abroad. And personalised number plates get up my nose. Spending all that money on saying, 'I am great!'

FIRST KISS:

I'm still looking for it... no. The first real snogging tonsil tester was in the second year when I was 13. Her name was Yvette Jones and she was in my class. She was being harassed by other guys and I was the knight in shining armour who walked her back to the house. She said thanks and stuck her tongue down my throat. I was paralysed. I had no idea that was what happened. I went home whistling.

FRIGHTENING MOMENT:

I had a bad motorbike crash when I was 17. I was racing with another guy and flew off the road into a brick wall. I broke four ribs, smashed an arm and burst my spleen. They took me to hospital and I was on the critical list for two weeks. About a month afterwards, some mates took me out for the night and, as we came back, we hit a kerbstone, a tyre blew and we turned right over. It was an estate car with a dog guard. I flew out of the car and that was very frightening. It was a bad month.

FIRST BONK:

I was 15 and I was scared – it was the ultimate

mixture of pleasure and pain. You always have at the back of your mind that it's wrong and then: 'OH MY GOD!' It was exciting but extremely amateur – in her house, I think.

NORMAN PACE

NAME:
Norman John Pace

NICKNAME:
Gareth calls me 'The prat whose career I have carried for the last 20 years' or Norm for short. Also Norri and Namron because that's Norman backwards.

BORN:
17 February 1953 in Dudley, Worcestershire. My parents were Kathleen and Norman Pace. They split up when I was four, but I was so young it wasn't much of a problem.

SCHOOL:

First was Bishop Alexander in Newark, Notting-hamshire – where I was brought up. Then to Magnus Grammar when I was ten. Because I was a Catholic, I didn't have to go to assembly. So my cousin and I used to hang around in the classroom while they all went. One morning, he told me he knew how to make black eyes by rubbing charcoal around the eye socket and everyone would say, 'Cor, you've got a black eye, you must be 'ard.' But we had to use a black crayon, which we took from the teacher's desk, and I was done for stealing. I was distraught and in floods of tears. I was fairly reasonable academically, good at maths and French. But I was never outstanding at anything, which is the story of my life. I could do a bit of everything quite well, which I do now in our sketches.

JOBS:

I was a paperboy and rode a big grocer's bike like Norman Wisdom. The first day I fell off and smashed all the groceries. I was told, 'Once more and you're out, pal.' My mum was a waitress and used to get me jobs in the kitchens paying five bob an hour, which was great. I also worked in a glue factory – I was stuck there for a while. Every morning, I would cycle there and you could smell it from two miles away – disgusting. But after eight hours of that I used to fly home feeling very happy...

CAREER:

I was always on stage, I couldn't wait to perform. Unfortunately, I've been married 15 years now and the opposite is true! I stood out in class because I could act and I performed just about all the starring roles. I wanted to go to acting college but Mum wanted me to be a teacher because it was more secure. When I met Gareth, he had always lived in London and he knew cool things like paying for a train fare. I wore a suit and tie on my first day at Avery Hill College Of Education. I walked into this room and there he was. He had a beard like Shaggy from *Scooby Doo*. He thought he was Bob Dylan – he'd introduce himself as Gareth Zimmerman – which he's now changed to Gareth Zimmerframe. My first thought was: 'Why have they put me a room with a man who can grow facial hair?' He said, 'So where you from then?' I said Newark and he replied, 'I'm from London.' I said what's your name, and he said Gareth. I said, 'Gary,' and he said, 'No, NEVER call me Gary ever. But you can call me Garth if you like.' Then I had to admit I was called Norman. But, after a week of sharing a room, we were getting on great because we shared a sense of humour and we both did PE together. In 1974, we started redoing folk songs and making them funny. Our first break in telly came when we gave up teaching and went for it in 1978.

FRIGHTENING MOMENT:

I hate performing to audiences who haven't come to see you specifically. When you walk out at the London Palladium and see mink coats and middle-aged people at the *Variety Show*, you think, 'Oh no, they won't understand our jokes or the tone of our humour.' We had to be very careful not to offend anyone. On a more serious note, though, my daughter had meningitis when she was born and had several emergency brain operations at Gt. Ormond Street Hospital. She suffered cerebral irritation during the procedure and, for six hours, she screamed the place down. We thought she was going to die. She had the maximum painkillers and sedatives and she was still kicking her feet and screaming. That was two months into the illness and it was so distressing that I had to leave the hospital. But, thank God, she recovered.

GREATEST MOMENT:

Nothing can beat being at a birth, because your emotions are at fever pitch. I wasn't allowed to see the first birth because my wife had to have an emergency Caesarean. But the other two were brilliant. I timed them both so I didn't have to miss the football of course...

COCK-UP:

We were playing at Craven Working Men's Club in 1978 and we had to do two hours, but only had an hour's worth of material. After an hour, we said, 'That's all from us, we'll see you after the bingo.' But this bloke grabbed a mike and shouted, 'Oi – get back. There's no bingo on tonight.' So we had to do another half an hour of the same material. People started drifting away in their droves and we were dying a total death. It was awful. This booking agent, who'd come to see us perform, came up afterwards and told us, 'I've got to tell you, lads, you were codswallop.'

CAR:

The first was a powder-blue Fiat 850, which we went touring around Wales in. Sadly, the head gasket went and that was that. Now I drive a red 5 Series BMW.

HOLIDAYS:

Gareth, my wife and another friend Steve were given some tickets for a ferry trip to France and we drove around for three weeks in a car and went wherever we wanted. It was great.

DRINK:

I like real ale, good beer or malt whisky, which I collect at home.

MUSIC:
Pretty broad – from classical to heavy rock and everything in between. First record I bought was 'Daydream Believer' by The Monkees.

BOOK:
Bertrand Russell's *History Of Philosophy* and *Catch 22* by Joseph Heller.

ADMIRE:
Steve Martin. I would love to meet him, he's got such an immense gift but seems so down-to-earth.

HEIGHT:
5ft 7in.

HOBBIES:
Sport. Watching or playing – especially golf, skiing and cricket. I bought a satellite dish so I could watch more of it. I enjoy reading as well.

FILM:
Once Upon A Time In America. It was great value – three-and-a-half hours.

AMBITION:
To make a movie would be a great challenge. We've

never done anything that's lasted more than three minutes (ask my wife) and it would be nice to hold a part for longer than that (as she always says).

HATES:
Anything pretentious. People talking about catwalk clothes no one would ever wear make me vomit. I drive a BMW, but I wear jeans when I do it. So I'm not a poser!

WHO DO YOU FANCY:
Nine-and-a-half weeks with Kim Basinger would be great – in fact nine-and-a-half minutes would be – if I could last that long. Joanne Whalley is my favourite.

FIRST KISS:
Pamela Waterfall. I was ten and she was a very gushing young woman. It was a case of get your lips tightly together and push yourself hard against hers! It hurt. Then, when I was 14, I kissed this French girl. We'd been to the pictures and suddenly there was this great lump of damp sponge in my mouth. But I started to like it and realised I wasn't homosexual after all, which was a relief.

FRIGHTENING EXPERIENCE:
I used to be terrified of snakes until I met one in Australia and I quite liked it – he was my promoter!

I've had a couple of car accidents but I was fairly lucid at the time and nervous later.

FIRST BONK:
It happened in a house when I was 15. The girl was a year older and it was so clumsy and messy and awful that when we'd finished she was totally distraught and convinced she was pregnant because we'd taken no precautions. I thought, 'What have I done – this is the end of my life at 15. What will my mother say?' Then the next day her period began and I thought, 'GREAT – let's carry on.' I've done it three times since.

ROLF HARRIS

FULL NAME:
Rolf Harris. My mum christened me after an Aussie writer called Rolf Boulderwood.

NICKNAME:
Ris in High School – all the kids used to take the last syllable of your surname as in Har-RIS.

BORN:
30 March 1930. I'm an Aries. Born in Perth, West Australia. Mum is Agnes Margerie. Dad was Cromwell George. My brother Bruce manages me worldwide from Sydney.

SCHOOLS:

Bassendean Primary was the first. I was very good at drawing and acting but really bad at maths. My best subject was swimming. We lived by the river and I fell in when I was about three. It terrified the life out of my parents, who immediately taught me to swim and I became the best swimmer in the school. When I was 12, I arrived at this High School and they had a swimming sports day and I put my name down for every event. The sports master called me in and said it was not a funny joke but I insisted I could do it. I ended up winning the open all-ages freestyle event in my first year. It was unheard of. I got into the state championships and won the Australian Junior Backstroke Championships, which made me somewhat of a celebrity. But it didn't do my other academic studies much good. I remember getting six whacks across the backside with a cane for getting two sums right out of eight when everyone else got the lot right. I was so thrilled I went to the loo and showed all my bloody great weals to the other boys to prove how tough I was. Then I proudly showed my mum but she went up the wall and practically blew the head off the headmaster and threatened to murder the teacher concerned. I never fought – I hated physical violence and still do. And I couldn't stand Aussie Rules football. The only game I ever played, I got the ball and got trampled. The school hero asked me for the ball and I handed it to him instead of punching it. That was a foul and he was so disgusted he just threw the ball down and stormed off. I was so shattered that I never played again.

JOBS:

I was a postman for a while. And I also worked on a blue asbestos mine during the holidays. Forty years later, many of the people who worked there are dying from asbestosis. Nobody knew at the time. Ten years ago, I went for a test and that was a very scary business. I was clear but a lot of people near the actual crushing have died horrible deaths.

CAREER:

I used to play on the piano at home and muck around with the words. Then I won a talent show at 17 and that gave me the boost I needed. I played the piano in a jazz band and did a few gigs. Then I went to teachers' college and became a teacher, but I knew I was throwing away my artistic side so I went back to art school and did cabaret at night. I saved £297 and came to England. I thought it would last me forever, because it was a lot of money at the time. But it ran out in six months. Luckily, I got an audition doing cartoons on a TV show called *Jigsaw* in 1953. Then I did a song for EMI and it became a smash hit No 1 – 'Tie Me Kangaroo Down Sport'. It was the first song that anyone had done in a genuine Australian accent. It was considered a second-rate accent in those days. That record changed all that and now we have Paul Hogan and co.

GREATEST MOMENT:

Winning the Australian Junior Backstroke Championship was just amazing. I swam that race in my dreams for six months afterwards. Mum and Dad were there and it was magic. Another great moment was when I performed in 1979 at a concert to celebrate the 150th anniversary of the founding of Australia. I was invited back as the big star from England to perform and Mum and Dad were there. It was in my home town of Sydney and my parents loved it. Until then, they had always regarded showbiz as a second-rate affair, My dad and I sang the Gendarmes duet on stage accompanied by the West Australian Symphony Orchestra. That was a great moment. I have a recording of that and it's one of my most treasured possessions. My dad died a year later from asbestosis. He'd been working at the power station, all the hot water pipes were lagged with asbestos and one of the machines broke down. For a month, the air was grey with dust from these pipes and 40 years later it killed him from cancer of the lung. He had it at the time of the recording but nobody knew. That's why it's so special

COCK-UP:
In my year in Vancouver, I had an offer to go to a mason-like convention in Seattle and perform for them. I was sold as the sole entertainment for these people. But they couldn't understand a word I said and had never heard of England, let alone Australia. They looked totally blank. In the middle of my third song, this man stood up and said, 'Excuse me, young man' several times until I stopped singing. Then he said, 'We just don't know what you are talking about and we think you had better call it a day.' The others then all got up, said they agreed and walked slowly out. If I could have turned into a grease-spot and sunk through the floor at that point, I would have done. It was dreadful. But ten years later, I did a similar convention in Canada and killed them – that erased the awful moment.

CARS:
My first was a 1928 Singer, which cost me £100. It was navy blue but me and my dad painted it dark brown. I paid for it from the proceeds of an exhibition of paintings when I was 16. I painted a

nude woman on the back, who I called Chloe and the car became a landmark in the area! Now I have a Mercedes station wagon.

HOME:
A place by the river in Bray.

HOLIDAYS:
I don't like holidays. I like to do different things, like going to learn about furniture making or something. That would be a holiday for me. I like making things, I can't stand lying around sunbathing. I don't spend as much time with my wife Alwen as I would like to. Perhaps that's why we are still together – there's a lot to catch up on when we meet again after a break.

FOOD:
Curries are my favourite. I like Tandoori chicken and Kormas. I hate having my mouth blasted.

DRINK:
I don't drink much at all. Lager with a curry and ginger beer I suppose. One glass of white wine can give me a two-day headache so I can't see the point. I never drink before performing.

MUSIC:

I used to play old 78s on a wind-up gramophone. Val Doonican was the guy who I modelled myself on when I came to England – I loved his relaxed style and I tried to emulate him. He was my big role model, he still is even now. He could charm the birds off the trees. Harry Belafonte was a big hero of mine until I met him. He had no time for me really. I was on *The Ed Sullivan Show* and so was he. I went up and introduced myself and said I'd had a big hit in Aus with 'Tie Me Kangaroo'. He just turned his back and looked the other way. I thought, 'Oh dear.' I always remember his rudeness and treat my fans as kindly as I can. Perhaps I caught him on a bad day but he treated me like a nobody, a total snub. It was like: 'You're no one, piss off.' Typically American attitude. I went on the Andy Williams show to do a duet and he didn't rehearse it. I was told that Mr Williams doesn't rehearse. I said it was crazy but that was that. Then I was told Mr Williams didn't want to do the duet because he didn't know my angle, where I was coming from. What I wanted from him! I said I had no angle and that it was ridiculous. That summed it up to me. I ended up doing it with Jimmy Durante.

HOBBIES:
Taking photos.

HATES:

Unnecessary bad manners. Inconsiderate behaviour.

FIRST KISS:

I was 16 and it was in Sydney. I had taken this girl to a dance and I was so shy but head over heels in love with her. She'd been seeing this other guy so I asked him if I could take Hazel to this dance. He even offered to ask her for me, which he did. Then he asked how I was going to get home after the dance and suggested I stay at her place overnight, and he arranged that with her as well. I was so nervous. At the end of the dance, we caught the tram back to Perth, then to her place. We were walking down this path and I put my arm behind her after several attempts! My arm kept jumping around in mid-air. She dropped her head on my shoulder and it was like an electric shock – I let go of her and jumped a yard away. We completed the walk a yard apart. Then we got there and she kissed me. She showed me where to sleep, with her three brothers. And in the next room was her bed. I didn't sleep a wink. Holding hands lasted for three months before I progressed – it was just magic. Not knowing how far to go all the time...

FRANKIE HOWERD
1917-1992

FULL NAME:
Francis Alec Howard. Because there were so many Howards around in showbusiness – Leslie, Trevor, Sidney and all the rest – I decided to alter it slightly. I was going to change it altogether but I thought it would end up being a bit of a bother really. I thought also that people would remember me because I spelled my name wrong! It seemed to work.

NICKNAME:
Frankie.

BORN:
York. My father was a soldier called Frank, who

came down to Woolwich Barracks in South East London with my mum Edith and me. We were brought up in Eltham.

SCHOOL:

The Gordon's School, Eltham, named after the general. I was very obedient at school. When I was about ten, I won a scholarship to a grammar school. I was given 324 sums to do in my holiday to prove I was up to it, and I did them. The teacher didn't expect us to do the lot, but I was the only person who had. So I got the scholarship, not through brains but through hard work. I went to Shooters Hill Grammar School. When you think that I have no sense of business or finances at all now – yet then I was a maths expert. My worst subject was geography, appalling. Now I have travelled a lot, so it's very good! A complete turnaround really. I was quite a good cricketer; I remember being cheered off the field at school for getting five people out in one over. I also did school plays and became the backbone of the group. I specialised in the comedy parts, and was considered to be a bit of a star, which made me feel this was going to be my career and life. I was always a bit outrageous and anarchical. My reports would always say I was very good at drama. I've still got them.

CAREER:

My first performance was bottom of the bill in a variety show at the Sheffield Empire. I got nine minutes.

GREATEST MOMENT:

I've had a very varied career. Playing in Buckingham Palace was wonderful – but so was the Borneo Jungle. And so can be playing to old age pensioners or children. They are all great moments. Every show is THE most important show as far as I am concerned. I want every audience to enjoy it as much as the last one.

COCK-UP:

I topped the bill at the London Palladium soon after Danny Kaye and they celebrated this incredible honour by putting my name up on huge hoardings. It was successful so I was asked to do the Royal Command Performance. I followed Billy Cotton's very popular jazz band. They were very noisy and they should have closed the show. But I had to follow them like a drizzle following a typhoon. I died on my feet, because I'd been given such a build-up. I was devastated. I'd died in front of the King and Queen, I walked around outside and got back in time for the finale. Then I did something very stupid. I told the press that I was very depressed about my performance. I remember it vividly because it was the first big public failure I'd had and it affected me very much. But eventually I realised it was part of showbusiness. It was traumatic but it taught me a lesson. I'd been overhyped. I don't get too down when things go wrong these days.

HOLIDAYS:
Deep-sea fishing on the Great Barrier Reef in Australia. There were sharks and God knows what else.

FOOD:
I like most food if it is reasonably plain, not smothered in sauce. Steak and kidney pies, marmalade, sponge puddings. Roast beef and lamb, stodgy but nice. I often go out for Indian and Chinese food as well.

DRINK:
Gin and tonics are my favourite tipple at a social event. Otherwise mineral water.

ADMIRE:
Max Miller, Jimmy James and the greatest of all was Sid Field to my mind. He was just extraordinary on stage – magnetic. I don't need to tell anyone who's good and who's not. I admire survivors, people who are still successful 30 years after they started. What I like now is that all the kids seem to know me – that's great. I love children.

GLORIA HUNNIFORD

FULL NAME:
Gloria Mary Winnifred Hunniford. A lot of people think it's a stage name but it isn't. When my husband told his family he was marrying me, they said, 'No wonder – she wants to change her name!' My married name is Keating, which my daughter Caron uses. I was stopped for speeding not long ago and, when the policeman saw my licence, it said Mary W. G. Keating. He looked at it and asked me if it was right! He was trying to connect it to the face but couldn't and I certainly wasn't going to help him. It can be quite useful at times having another name on official documents.

NICKNAME:

I never had one, until I worked for Ulster TV when I was 19 and they called me Honey. Then Larry Grayson tagged me Glo when we appeared together on TV and that seems to have stuck. Terry Wogan used to call me Grievous Bodily and Gus Honeybun. Terry helped me enormously by doing that – and by continually referring to my black stockings and suspenders.

BORN:

10 April, 1 a.m., very typical Aries. Mum was called May and Dad Charles, known as Charlie, was a magician. I have a younger brother called Charles, and a sister born on my birthday seven years before me.

SCHOOL:

Church St. Primary in Portadown, County Armagh, Northern Ireland. I was always being slung out of class for talking. And I had tongue-tie, like my grandfather, my father and my son Michael now. I had it snipped. Mum said on TV recently that she wasn't sure if that was a good thing! I was captain of the hockey team, which came as a surprise to me, because I hated the game. My biggest claim to fame was that I won a competition for talking non-stop for more hours than anyone else.

CAREER:

My dad used to take me along to his magic shows and I sang the national anthem with him on stage when I was nine, which was my first live performance. It was great training for learning to play to audiences. They just don't bother me now. I went to Canada when I was 17 and got a request show on the local radio, then a TV slot. I was offered a job as a presenter when I was interviewed on radio about a record I did called 'Are You Ready For Love', which reached number seven in the Ulster charts, and the producer thought I could talk a lot. But I gave up singing because cabaret spots were being blown up all the time – it was too dangerous.

GREATEST MOMENT:

Having my children was wonderful. It was the best thing I have ever done in my life. And coming to London for the first time was great. I was invited to stand in for Jimmy Young and I arrived at the BBC building and it was terrifying. I thought, 'God, do I actually have to go through with this?'

COCK-UP:

I was doing a radio show at Broadcasting House in Northern Ireland. I'd torn all the ligaments in my leg but I managed somehow to get myself up the lift, up some stairs and into my studio. Then I had to tell this woman she'd won £250 in a contest and I came out with: 'The only problem is you should see my poor old producer grovelling around under my crutch looking for your prize.' Oh dear!

CARS:

My first car was a green Mini Traveller, a fabulous car which I bought off my best girlfriend Ann Thompson. I scrimped and saved and my uncle in Canada gave me £100 towards the £300. It was a fortune for me at the time but I carried babies, garden seats, everything in it. I now have a Rover Vitesse.

HOME:

I live in Sevenoaks. We had a huge fire last year and that was awful. Although it was contained to the hall, everything was smoke-ridden. I love that house, and love going home there. You have to be happy when you close the front door and I am.

HOLIDAYS:

The Seychelles. I went there two years ago and want to go back. It's idyllic.

FOOD:

I like really exotic seafood, like lobster. It's a treat.

DRINK:

I like Champagne but I've given up drink for two months at the moment. So I'm drinking lots of water.

MUSIC:

I like most things, though I lean towards Frank Sinatra, and middle-of-the-road standards. My first record was 'Take Five' by Dave Brubeck – a great record. My best album would be the Domingo, Carreras and Pavarotti live show. It was such a wonderful atmosphere, I would never get tired of that record. I like Julio Iglesias and Barry Manilow as well.

ADMIRE:

My favourite broadcaster would be Alastair Cooke. He wove such lovely stories in his *Letter From America* show and has a wonderful voice which transports you from the kitchen sink to America. Terry Woman was just unsurpassed on radio. He had it down to a fine art – just classic.

HOBBIES:

Tennis, when I don't break my arm.

FILMS:

Gone With The Wind and *Breakfast At Tiffanys*. I watch

Gone With The Wind when I've had an argument – I iron furiously for four hours watching it!

AMBITION:
I want to do Alan Whicker's job – it's the best in the business.

HEIGHT:
5ft 2in.

HATES:
I can't stand shop assistants who stand around nattering and don't serve you. And I hate grocery shops that don't provide bags for your groceries. I have fought a campaign locally for that. I don't like people shouting at me either – it's so rude.

FRIGHTENING MOMENT:
The worst thing was breaking my shoulder. I never felt anything that painful before and I never want to again. I fell against this tennis net pole and it was the most excruciating pain I've ever had – worse than childbirth even. The doctor said, 'I have to tell you you have broken it really badly. You will be lucky to have 40 per cent use of that arm for the rest of your life.' Can you imagine hearing that? It was an awful moment.

FANCY:

I have never really had a fantasy man. No James Dean or anything. I fancy an interview with Frank Sinatra because he never gives them but I don't fancy him sexually. Richard Gere in *Pretty Woman* looked great and Tom Selleck's very attractive.

FIRST KISS:

I remember my first boyfriend at Church St. Primary and my first kiss was in the back row of the cinema. He was a cheapskate because he always arranged to see me *inside* the cinema! But he bought the dolly mixtures. I was eight years old – a young starter.

DON JOHNSON

FULL NAME:
Donald Wayne Johnson.

NICKNAME:
Don.

BORN:
15 December 1949. Flat Creek, Missouri. I was a real farm boy and a Sagittarius.

SCHOOL:
I was a mischievous kid and often bunked off school. My dad was a master mechanic and taught me how to hot-wire a car. So one day a friend of mine and I stole

one. We ended up wrecking the car when we hit a telegraph pole. My friend got locked away for it because he was older than me – I got a month in a detention centre a few months later for stealing another car. I was 15.

JOBS:

I got a job in a meat market, to pay the rent, when I left home at 16 – my job was to sucker customers who had been brought in by misleading advertising. Eventually, I saw a guidance counsellor and he got me on to a drama course and I had finally found something I loved.

CAREER:

I studied drama at the University Of Kansas. After two years or so, I was talent-spotted by MGM while in a play at the American Conservatory Theater, San Francisco. But the film they gave me, *The Magic Garden of Stanley Sweetheart*, bombed.

GREATEST MOMENT:

Getting married to Melanie Griffiths for the second time.

COCK-UP:

Doing drugs. In the '60s, I got heavily into dope and coke. I was lucky I stopped before I did any permanent brain damage. A lot of my friends still do a lot of drugs and I wish they wouldn't, although I don't preach. When I was at my worst, I remember coming out of a club toilet with cocaine all over my upper lip and bumping straight into Jimi Hendrix. He said, 'Man, you can't walk around with coke on your face,' and he wiped it off for me. I was thunderstruck.

CARS:
I drive a Ferrari GTS.

HOME:
I live in Miami – in a five-bed house by the sea.

HOBBIES:
Song-writing, golf, fishing, powerboat racing and skiing.

HOLIDAYS:
At home in Miami.

FOOD:
My all-time favourite food is Swiss almond vanilla ice cream. Nothing beats it.

DRINK:
I used to drink myself stupid but now all you will find in my fridge is Diet Coke and orange juice.

MUSIC:
In the early '70s, I bought myself a $20 guitar and it didn't take me long to realise that I was never going to be Eric Clapton. But I have always found music therapeutic. I once sang some stuff with Frank Zappa and we talked about recording together but it never worked out. To this day, I still see myself as more of a rocker than an actor.

ADMIRE:
Actors who stay at the top.

HEIGHT:
5ft 10in.

FRIGHTENING MOMENT:
There was one scene in *Miami Vice* where we had to explode a bomb and it went off far sooner than it should have done – right next to where I was standing. Amazingly, I got away with hardly a scratch.

FANCY:
Madonna – when I heard that she wanted to meet me, I sent her a bunch of roses with a message saying, 'With major lust, Don Johnson.'

FIRST KISS:
I can't remember.

FIRST BONK:
I was 12 years old when I first got laid. It was with the 17-year-old baby-sitter my mother had hired to look after me for the weekend! She was real pretty and certainly looked after me OK. I was supposed to be old enough to look after myself and obviously my mum was right about that. In those days, most nice girls didn't but older nice girls did and they were the ones I was interested in. I was still in my teens when I moved in with a 26-year-old cocktail waitress.

BOB MONKHOUSE
1928-2003

FULL NAME:
Robert Alan Monkhouse – Americans never get it right, they always call me Mongoose. If I'd had my wits about me, I would have changed it at the start. People like Ted Ray and Lulu had it right – think of the ink I would have saved on autographs.

NICKNAME:
Monkey at school. I wouldn't have minded so much, but I hadn't told them my surname was Monkhouse yet!

BORN:
1 June 1928, shortly after 2 a.m. in Beckenham, Kent. I am a perfect Gemini according to the experts.

Dad was Wilfred Adrian, Chairman of Monkhouse Glasscock Ltd., custard powder and jelly manufacturers to royalty. Quite seriously. His father, my grandfather, founded the company. They had several huge factories, and rivalled Birds in the custard business. Mum was Dorothy Muriel, known as Buddy. My aunt was Hammy. I never realised why until they both died and I found a chest of very old, short comedy films from America starring the duo Bud and Ham. I felt quite emotional when I imagined these two girls giggling at this duo and naming themselves after them. I have one older brother, John, who is a natural accountant, like my father. He worked for Lew Grade and signed some of my cheques when I worked for Anglia! I am innumerate, but an artist like my mother. She even had the same mole as me on her chin. Father was a very perceptive man. He predicted there was going to be a Second World War and moved the family down from London to Worthing, Sussex, on 2 September 1939. The very next day, we listened to Chamberlain making his famous speech.

SCHOOL:
St Margaret's Infants School in Beckenham, Kent. Then the Grange School, run by a headmaster called Mr Beater, which was really asking for it, wasn't it!

Goring Hall Prep School, Sussex, during the war. Then, in 1942, we moved back to Beckenham, and I went to Dulwich College. I was very unsporting, still am. I neither played nor watch it. I don't like physical exertion or competitive sport. This was very difficult at a school where it was compulsory. I was very devious though. I developed a wonderful limp and got a note from a puzzled doctor who said I had some obscure disease of the knee. My personal Lourdes was West Dulwich Station. I would limp, hopelessly crippled, to and from it every day – only to be miraculously cured when I arrived home. I was never a fighter, never beaten, never any homosexual experiences. But I did get caught cheating. I took the Higher School Certificate a year early. I used a secret crib for the Latin exam, written on the inside of an eye patch. The Latin master found out and I was so overcome with mortification that I have never cheated since. I couldn't look at myself in the mirror for months afterwards. I couldn't face my parents either. They never forgave me – and didn't forgive me for going into showbusiness either.

JOBS:
I used to do cartoons when I was 12 and sell them to magazines. I sold my first one to *Mickey Mouse Weekly*. Then I drew a lot of strips for kids' magazines and I still

do a lot of cartoons now. I also wrote short stories for children. I was a cheap writer, I got a florin, that was 10p, for 2,000 words. I churned them out throughout my adolescence on my old Imperial typewriter with two fingers. My first salaried job was as an animator for some of Walt Disney's top men nicked by J. Arthur Rank to rival Disney. It never worked.

CAREER:
I started by standing up at school concerts, telling jokes and writing school comedies. Then I joined various drama groups. Someone offered me five pounds to compere a peace rally in Beckenham. I was working as a freelance reporter for the *Beckenham Journal* at the time. I was bitten by the bug immediately. I was called up to the RAF soon afterwards. I was ground crew, very lowly. I came out a corporal. I applied to the BBC for an audition towards the end. I forged a letter from my boss saying, if I didn't get an audition, it would probably affect my mental balance. I got a reply within two days giving me an audition! Luckily, the old guy, who had tested for 22 years and savaged almost everyone, was ill that day and they let a new young man audition me. I started telling jokes and kept going for ten minutes and he wrote, '101 per cent – wow!' The BBC sent my warrant officer a note saying I was a genius. I got

offered five broadcasts, which people would have given their bollocks for, and I became an almost overnight radio star. Then I did the variety touring circuit and wrote scripts for radio shows. At one point, I and a colleague wrote 19 shows a WEEK, including everything from *Hello Playmates* for Arthur Askey to *OK The Saucy Boy* for Radio Luxembourg. I was the Tescos of comedy! Then I got offered my first TV show, *Fast And Loose*. I was offered the chance to call it *The Bob Monkhouse Show* but said no. That was a big mistake – ever since, I have had the name Bob in the title somewhere! I did a load of comedy movies in the late '50s as well. Now I do a lot of corporate shows – in a typical week I've done Data Point, Mars Bars, Mazda Cars, a nightclub called Victoria's. I work hard, but I enjoy it. My wife says I'm not a workaholic, but an alcoholic. If I watch *Cheers* and hear a line I like, I replay it again and again until I work it into something I can use. I look at Bob Hope and think I want to be where he is when I'm 80. He's never lost his motivation.

I was upset when Les Dawson took over *Opportunity Knocks*. He's a wonderful comedian, and I love him very much, but I just don't think he enjoys the show as much as I did and that makes me sad. I have never, ever thought about the money while working. It's nice to see the cheque afterwards but it's not the motivation. I tried as hard when I earned 10 bob a week from the BBC as I do now.

FRIGHTENING MOMENT:

I was doing *The Bob Monkhouse Show* and Pamela Stephenson was one of my guests. She came on to the set clutching this pistol. I thought it was a joke but I said, 'Pamela, what on earth are you doing?' She just laughed and told me not to worry about it. It was just a little trick she'd learned with a pistol. 'They're only blanks.' At that point, she fired it and shattered a window by the side of the stage. I was sure it was a real bullet and I thought she had cracked up, gone mad. But it turned out she'd carefully set up detonators around, which went off at the prearranged time. Very clever... but very frightening.

GREATEST MOMENT:

I promised my kids I wouldn't mention them so that excludes those wonderful moments with them. But I think building my own home in St James, Barbados, is the highlight of my life. I stood on a patch of beach there three years ago and thought it was paradise. So I bought the land and now I've built my own three-storey dream house. A few weeks ago I stood on the third floor, looked down through the palm trees over the Caribbean and I thought, 'Jesus, all those sweaty toilets I've lumbered about in, with my make-up running under my bow tie and, that's all added up to this.' I know I've got.a lovely home, a lovely car and a nice pension, but I think opening our first bottle of Champagne at our new home in Barbados was the realisation of a 30-year career dream. We've called it Sandcastle, though I wanted to call it Punters, because they've paid for it! Another great moment was discovering Paul Newman was only 5ft 2in.

COCK-UP:

I have some very nasty heckler-stoppers. I don't like saying the old cliches like: 'Sit by the wall, that's plastered as well.' If someone says, 'Drop Dead,' I reply, 'You first.' Some intelligent hecklers can make great live comedy. But I began to think I was the master of heckling, and would invite drunks to have a go at me so I could take the piss out of them. I remember the Cavendish Club in Sheffield – it was MY room. I was the favourite act there and I was riding cocaine-high. They loved me. It was safe. Then I did this show there and one guy, very drunk, said something abusive. I jumped down, went over to him and asked him to repeat it, which he did. I couldn't make out what he was saying so I gave him some fearful stick and the crowd lapped it up – at that moment, I was totally in charge. I could have walked on water, cured lepers, anything. Then a guy with this bloke said to me, 'He's only trying to tell you he loves you, Mr Monkhouse – he's handicapped.'

CARS:
My first car was a 1936 Ford Popular. Now I drive two 560 Mercedes, one SL, the other SE.

HOME:
A 14th-century farmhouse in Leighton Buzzard, Bedfordshire.

HOLIDAYS:
Barbados. My wife Jackie and I have been six or seven times and we love it. I take 40 books and read two a day.

FOOD:
Steak and kidney pie, mash, roast spuds and peas. Or roast pheasant Normandie with apples and cream.

DRINK:
18-year-old MacAllan malt whiskey. It is unbelievable. The 10-year-old is like listening to an orchestra, the 18-year-old adds the string section. Otherwise, Diet Coke.

ADMIRE:
Ben Elton, Rowan Atkinson, French and Saunders, Steve Martin. I saw Peter Sellers and Terry Thomas storm to superstardom and I stood back and watched and said, 'Wow, look at that.'

HEIGHT:
6ft.

BOOK:
I enjoyed Idi Amin's cookery book, *How To Serve Your Fellow Man*.

HOBBIES:
Reading and relaxing in the sun. I love researching comedy – I collect jokes by the thousand.

FILM:
Buster Keaton in *Sherlock Junior*.

AMBITION:
To carry on as I am.

FRIGHTENING EXPERIENCE:
I can't swim. Water is my deepest fear ever since I almost drowned as a child. I was five and I was playing around in this strawberry farm in Kent. I ran about

whooping and yelling and ran straight into a cesspit. I was hysterical when they finally got me out – I couldn't speak for a week. I've hated water ever since.

HATES:

Somebody who gets in between me and getting a laugh. The guy who forgets a key prop, the guy who edits a crucial line, the pianist who hits the keyboard on the punchline.

FANCY:

Raquel Welch in *The Hunchfront of Notre Dame*...

FIRST KISS:

I was 15. It was terrific. It was my aunt Renee. She was drunk, and wonderful. It led to the total experience, it was great.

VIC REEVES

FULL NAME:
Jim Moir. I changed it to Vic Reeves because that sounded more showbiz. It was genuinely the first name that came into my head. Another factor was that the Head of BBC Light Entertainment is also called Jim Moir.

NICKNAME:
Vic.

BORN:
I was born in Darlington, which is even more boring than Middlesbrough. I moved to London as soon as I could to escape.

SCHOOL:

I trained to be an aircraft engineer but I didn't have the dedication for it. I was a mechanical inspector and was expected to get up really early, looking bright and chirpy, for a hard day's work on the plane. But that meant I couldn't go boozing every night so I packed it in.

JOBS:

I was a pig-farmer for a while. I swilled out 100 pigs and 40 cattle for two years. I had to change clothes after work and take frequent showers but still stank to high heaven. They wouldn't let me on the bus so I had to cycle home on an old bike after every shift. I was also a singer in a punk band, a painter and a compulsive liar, of course.

CAREER:

I started off in local London pubs causing havoc with carrots and things like that. One of the regulars was a solicitor called Bob Mortimer who kept offering suggestions for my act, until we decided to save time and become a double act. After a few months, I was asked by a mate if I would help him run a comedy club at the Goldsmith's Tavern in Deptford, South London. We couldn't get any acts so I went on myself all the time. I got my first TV break when Jonathan Ross asked me on to *Last Resort*. I used to run a club with his brother, Adam, and we all went out to dinner one night where I presented him with some pen and ink sketches I'd done. They got me on the show.

DANGEROUS MOMENT:

I almost blew my hand off doing a gunpowder stunt for the *Big Night Out*. I was doing this gag with an oven, which I intended to blow up. I put a load of gunpowder inside and went to light a match but then it exploded at the wrong moment. I burned all the skin off my hand and was in agony. But I had to continue without letting the audience know what had happened. I cut short the act and went to hospital in the break! On another occasion, I was doing a routine with a comedian called Price Slasher and, during the scene, his hand slipped and he knifed me by mistake. I've still got the blood-soaked script.

COCK-UP:

We did a video for my first pop song, a cover version of 'Born Free'. I made it with a pack of council-estate dogs but, when we put them on a podium with me, they started having minor indiscretions all over the place.

CARS:

I have formed a Gentleman's Motorcycle Club with Bob Mortimer and Jools Holland. We have all got vintage bikes and every Sunday we put on our tweeds, smoke pipes and drive them. We have an initiation ceremony based on the Hells Angels – they have to eat live chickens. With us, new members have to take us out for a chicken curry.

HOME:
North London

DRINK:
I can't drink much – after the first eight pints I find it tough going, and I stay off really strong lagers.

MUSIC:
I have a big classical collection. All proles do – go into any prole's house on an estate and you'll find a bit of Beethoven stashed away there. I used to be in a punk band called Hot Murder in 1984. We did three gigs and played our own songs like 'Help A Little Child Across The Road Of Death'.

ADMIRE:
I always loved Eric Morecambe, he was just slightly cruel which was great. We don't copy him, but he was a great inspiration to many comics.

HATES:

Panto and chat shows. I went on Gloria Hunniford's show and it was a terrible experience. A ghastly nightmare and I'm not going to do any more of that.

FRIGHTENING MOMENT:

I got a terrible attack of vertigo on a fairground big wheel ride. I'm petrified of heights anyway, and when we stopped at the top I got this irresistible urge to jump. I would almost certainly have been killed if I'd tried but Bob Mortimer grabbed me at the last minute and talked me back to sense. I will never go on one again – I find heights terrifying. That was the most frightening moment of my life.

WENDY RICHARD

NAME:
Wendy Richard. When Mother christened me, she did it short so I could fit it into cheques!

NICKNAME:
Wendy M, I hate being called Wend. Mum would turn in her grave if she heard that because she wanted a name for me that wouldn't be shortened.

BORN:
20 July 1943. I'm a Cancer, the nicest sign of the Zodiac. I was born in a pub, the Corporation Hotel in Middlesbrough. We moved to London pretty quickly, to the Shepherds Market area in Mayfair.

SCHOOL:

St George's in Mount Street, Streatham, and the Royal Masonic School for Girls in Rickmansworth. My first day was terrible, I felt such a little soul going into this huge building. I didn't think I would ever get out. I was naughty but not wicked. We were all very innocent in those days. I scrumped lots of apples. I was sent home once from nursery school for biting other kids.

JOBS:

My first job was in the fashion department at Fortnum and Mason, where I got three shillings and fourpence a week.

CAREER:

Mum sent me to the Italia Conti Drama School. I was run over on my first day. I had 22 stitches in my forehead, and ten in the back of my head. Someone rang Mum and told them I was dead. She turned up at the hospital in tears.

My first part was in a TV show with Sammy Davis Jnr., I was with Mandy Rice-Davis. We were the glamour. He was wonderful. A real gent. I was in *Dad's Army* as a cinema usherette – it was like being in a private gentlemen's club, they were all lovely. I remember Arnold Ridley looking for his stage mark to stand on, and he said, 'It's like an old warthog looking for a place to die.'

Are You Being Served? came along in 1972. It was great fun. I remember doing the stage play. Molly Sugden had to make her entrance and she had to show off some Union Jack knickers and that got the laugh. Then one night she forgot and hadn't got any knickers on. I was helpless with laughter.

GREATEST MOMENT:

Two years ago, I got the Northern TV personality award. I flew up to Newcastle. Not many people know that I'm a Geordie and, when we got to the venue and they read my name, I couldn't speak. It meant so much to me. I then won all the prizes in the raffle! I gave them away though.

COCK-UP:

When Julia Smith got the idea for *EastEnders*, they rang my agent and asked me to read for them. I saw this guy and he asked me what I'd done, and I replied, 'What, you mean today?' They didn't know I was a Geordie!

CAR:

I have failed my test six times and given up.

HOME:
West End.

HOLIDAYS:
Singapore, and the Great Barrier Reef and we went to Hawaii – for a delayed honeymoon last year – it was brilliant.

FOOD:
Curry. I would happily eat it every night, the best I've done is five times in one week.

DRINK:
Must have a good cuppa in the morning and then some Champagne later.

MUSIC:
I don't like pop music. I'm into classical at the moment. The first record I bought was 'I Thought I Saw A Pussycat'.

ADMIRE:
Albert Finney – I did *Gumshoe* with him, and he was a sweetheart. And I love Maggie Smith. We met at a health farm recently in the sauna! There was us two, Sylvia Syms and Elspeth Grey all in the same Turkish bath.

HEIGHT:
I'm 5ft 5in.

HOBBIES:
I love gardening and watching things grow. I did everything in red, white and blue in the window-boxes for the Queen Mum's 90th. Now, for my husband's birthday, I'm doing everything in gold and green.

AMBITION:
To be in *The Archers* – I'm an addict.

FILM:
Seven Brides For Seven Brothers and *West Side Story*.

BOOK:
Tom Sharpe is brilliantly funny. If you see someone reading a book and laughing out loud, it's one of his.

HATES:
Litter and people who drive their cars with their windows open and their radios blaring – that is so rude.

FANCY:
Sean Connery and Albert Finney.

FIRST KISS:

I was very nervous and extremely naive. He asked if I was a virgin and I said, 'Certainly not, I'm Church of England.' I was 15 and he took me straight home.

FRIGHTENING MOMENT:

When I came home and found my mother collapsed on the floor. I have no brothers or sisters and I thought, 'Oh God, I'm going to be left on my own.' But, when I did lose her, I learned to look after myself.

BEST PARTY:

The day I married Paul. The sun was shining, it was St Patrick's Day and everyone had a good time.

JONATHAN ROSS

FULL NAME:
Jonathan Stephen Ross. I was called Stephen after the black sheep of the family, Uncle Steve, who I still keep in touch with. Mum says she called me Jonathan because she thought it would sound good if I made it in TV – and how right she was!

NICKNAME:
Wossy, normally, and Ross The Toss occasionally.

BORN:
17 November 1960. I was born at my parents' flat in Camden Town, North London. Apparently, my two older brothers were in the room with my dad at the

time – so it was a good old family affair. They clapped when I came out – I've never had such a good reception since.

SCHOOL:

My first school was David Lane Infants round the corner from our house in Leytonstone, East London. I remember on my first day seeing a rather attractive girl I will call Mary and thinking, 'Hey this is all right!' I was four at the time and she was five. I was so smitten that I presented her with a black ribbon for her hair. But I have to be honest, I was two-timing her with Kay Gillingham in the same class. Sadly, I had no luck with either of them. Mary later moved in with the local tough kid and had a child when she was about 11 or something! I used to get into trouble a lot at school. Fighting and generally upsetting teachers. I was caned a few times – but that wasn't too bad, I'd pay for that these days. I managed to pass English and history A levels, which got me into the only university that would have me – The School of Slavonic and East European Studies. It was a great place. I remember skipping three weeks of a History and Political Ideas course and, when the teacher asked me where I'd been, I thought, 'Oh sod it,' and replied, 'I've been in the park drinking wine.' After a few very delicate minutes, he replied, 'I respect your honesty – you may stay.' So I pulled that one off. I ended up with a 2.2 in East European Modern History. It comes in handy when I slip in tricky questions about Poland in 1660.

JOBS:

I had loads of daft jobs. I was a milk boy for many years, then I went to the fruit shop and delivered fruit on a clapped-out old bike. I would like to apologise now to my boss for not appearing every fourth weekend on some spurious excuse. The reason was that there was a local comic convention every month and I wouldn't have missed those for all the fruit in Leytonstone.

CAREER:

I had done TV ads when I was young, and when my brother, Paul, became a researcher for LWT I thought it sounded a very good idea. I wrote to hundreds of TV companies and amazingly got a job at Channel Four, I was dead lucky. I had no bank account but suddenly I was earning £260 a week. I remember taking my first pay packet home, spreading it out on the floor and looking at it for hours. I still do that these days, though I'm happy to say it covers a bit more ground. I never wanted to go on screen but then we devised this barmy talk show called *The Last Resort* and that was it. The rest, unfortunately for the viewers, is history.

FRIGHTENING MOMENT:

It used to be every night before *The Last Resort*. It was real skin-of-the-teeth stuff throughout the show and I had no experience of it. The worst show for nerves was when I interviewed Steve Martin. He was my all-time hero and I was scared stupid of making a prick of myself. As it turned out, I made a partial prick of myself by giggling all the way through it. Another little knee-trembler was when Jane took me on this freefall fairground ride in America, which terrified the life out of me. They just take you up in this thing pretending to be a parachute and drop you. There was no element of fun involved – except for looking at the big fat German tourist in the cage next to me who, because of his immense bulk, fell twice as fast as we did. But it was awful, the most unpleasant thing you can do to yourself. There was also a rather appalling plane journey in Mexico when we hit a tornado. I thought, 'Oh dear we're all going to die – can I have another drink, love?'

GREATEST MOMENT:

Meeting the *Coronation Street* star Chris Quinten... No, seriously, probably getting married. I didn't think it would be because I'd lived with Jane for a while, but when you actually say those immortal words: 'I do,' or as I said it: 'I'll give it my best shot,' then it gets to you. It's the public admission of love and respect. But I guess the birth of my first child was the best highlight.

COCK-UP:
Back to the birth of my first child... No, I guess interviewing Sarah Miles and making a real pig's ear of it. I asked her if she drinks her own urine, which she does, and she just looked at me and said, 'Why, do you eat your own shit?' There was a hush of deathly tones, it was awful. Everyone had tuned in because of all the press I'd got from the first show. John Hurt was another terrible show, he seemed to be pissed in a very non-entertaining way.

CARS:
My first car was a Vauxhall Astra convertible. I didn't learn to drive until I was 27, after I'd started *The Last Resort*. Now I have a Mazda RX7 and Jane's got a Mazda MX5. I also have a Mazda 626 for the family. You could say I like Mazdas.

HOME:
First home was a small one-bed flat in Holland Road, Shepherd's Bush. It was a pain in the arse because people always rang the intercom, and the lights were always breaking. But I did well out of it. It cost me

£51,000 and I sold it for £75,000. My new home is in Hampstead, NW3.

HOLIDAY:

My favourite holiday was at a little place in Sardinia. It was a small hotel with a pool, a beach and nothing else. You could literally do nothing all day and night. Normally, I go somewhere really expensive where you hire a car, run around like mad seeing everything and feel knackered when you get back. But this one was great.

FOOD:

I'm going on a diet soon because I've put on too much weight. I like all food: Indian, Thai, Japanese, Mexican, English, Italian – food in vast amounts basically. If I'm treating Jane, we go to Blake's Hotel, which costs an arm and your bollocks, but it's great.

DRINK:

I like white wine and bottled lager. But I've had some bad experiences on the sauce. One of the worst was when I was 16 and my brother was getting married to an Irish girl. All her family came over and we all piled down to the local pub with them. I had just started drinking, cider of course, and I downed eight pints like there was no tomorrow. Then I threw up inside the pub. The whole place was silenced by the appalling sight and sound of this young man vomiting profusely in the corner. But I finished what I was doing and went up to the bar to order another pint. My brothers-in-law were absolutely horrified. The other time was an all-day-and-night binge with a friend of mine called Alan, which finished at four in the morning. Unfortunately, I was due to keep score during a pilot for a new Jeremy Beadle show the next morning. I wasn't capable of keeping my bloody breakfast down, let alone keeping score.

MUSIC:
All sorts – in my car at the moment I've got everything from *Anthony Newley's Greatest Hits* to Tone Loc's rap LP. I love old Roxy Music and David Bowie stuff. It's nostalgia for me now.

BOOK:
Pale Fire by Nabokov.

ADMIRE:
Steve Martin, Russ Meyer, Frankie Howerd, lots of film directors, Martin Amis, Tony Benn, because he's stuck with his views, Maggie Thatcher for the same reasons, Chris Tarrant, my mum and dad for bringing us all up so brilliantly.

HEIGHT:
7ft 7in, but on TV I look about 6ft 1in.

HOBBIES:
Collecting comics – I've got tens of thousands now, which I will sell off one day in the all-time great comic sale.

FILM:
It's A Wonderful Life, *The Jerk*, *2001*, *Dawn of the Dead*, *Beetlejuice* and *Citizen Kane*, of course.

AMBITION:
I would like one day to have finished paying the mortgage.

FRIGHTENING EXPERIENCE:
Weighing myself after my first trip to Miami. I was about 14-and-a-half stone and it scared the life out of me. A serious moment, though, came when I had a car crash in Los Angeles. An airport van hit me in the back and turned me towards a parked car. I swerved up on to a pavement at 70mph and I was so panicked I stopped and put the windscreen wipers on! Jane was in the car with me and it was very scary. Both cars were written off, but we escaped without a scratch. We could have been killed if I had braked rather than swerved.

FANCY:

The wife of course; Dawn French, all of her, and Barbara Windsor.

FIRST KISS:

It was with an Irish girl after the reception at my brother's wedding. I was 16 – older than I should have been. I don't remember her name – isn't that terrible? I remember giggling because it was all rather curious and having to persuade her that someone was pulling faces behind her.

FIRST BONK:

A girl I lived with before Jane. It was fairly nice. I remember smiling for some time before, during and afterwards. I was about 21 at the time.

EMMA SAMMS

FULL NAME:
Emma Samuelson.

NICKNAME:
Sometimes I get called Sam for obvious reasons. When we were kids, my sister Louise would call me Emu, because I had long legs, I guess.

SCHOOL:
I went to the Royal Ballet School, it was a very unusual school. There were less than 150 pupils there, ranging from the ages of 11 to 16. It was a co-educational boarding school. We did an average of four hours' dancing every day, as well as academic work. My

speciality was choreography. I think I would have ended up doing that, if things hadn't turned out differently. I did some dancing in the movie I did with John Candy, called *Delirious*. And that was really the first time I had danced on camera, so all those years of training finally paid off. I can still do the splits and a full backbend, which was useful because we did this amazing dance number, a Fred and Ginger-style routine with lifts and spins.

JOBS:

I used to sometimes work the switchboard for my father's company in the school holidays and I remember being quite an expert at cutting people off, especially if they were on long-distance calls. Nowadays, I'm a partner with my father, Michael, in his lighting company, Samuelson Lighting. My first showbiz job was a print advert for Polaroid, which we did in Greece when I was 17. The photographer on the shoot realised it was my first job, because halfway through the shoot he said, 'You're not enjoying this at all.' I didn't like having my picture taken.

BREAK:

Arabian Adventure, a movie with Oliver Tobias, Christopher Lee and Mickey Rooney. I was with an agent when I was 17 years old, and I had admitted to him that I had no acting experience or training. The first audition he sent me to was for the female lead in this big EMI feature film. I did a screen test and got the part, to everyone's amazement, including my agent.

CAREER:

I moved to the States in 1980. I had a small one-roomed apartment in a part of Los Angeles called Westwood. I got a job as a waitress in a delicatessen. Then I got a role in a mini-series with Mark Hamon, called *Goliath Awaits*.

After that, I got a part in *General Hospital*, which was the number-one daytime soap opera in America. I auditioned about five times to get the job, it was a very gruelling audition process.

I used to have to memorise 30 pages of dialogue every day. I think I still hold the record for memorising the most dialogue in one day on *General Hospital*, which was 86 pages. I played the part of Holly. Things were going wrong all the time. We used to memorise our lines and look at the scripts right until the very last moment, and then we would hide the pages of dialogue all over the set. So what you never did was to move a piece of furniture or prop because, if you did, there was nearly always some mad panic and flurries of paper everywhere as actors searched for their scripts.

Then I was offered the part of Fallon in *Dynasty*. I ended up doing both shows at the same time for three months. The two characters had totally different hair colours. Fallon had red hair and Holly was a brunette, so running between jobs was made that much more difficult. When I first joined the cast of *Dynasty*, I kept my head down and tried to fit in. I made some very good friends there, mostly with the crew rather than the actors. I remember John Forsythe used to joke that he was the only one in the cast who didn't wear a wig! Now I and the rest of the cast of *Dynasty*, including Joan Collins and John Forsythe, are working on a four hour mini-series to show what happened to the characters after the end of the last series. I promise there will be some great surprises and the usual cliff-hangers that *Dynasty* fans have come to expect.

BIGGEST CHALLENGE:
When I had to go to New Zealand, over a year ago, to make a movie, I knew I was going to be there for four months, and I knew I wasn't going to know anyone. I had a similar experience in Hungary; I had to learn to take care of myself.

STARLIGHT FOUNDATION:
My cousin and I co-founded it eight years ago. It's a

charity that grants wishes to children who are critically, chronically or terminally ill. I was inspired to do it because I had a brother who died of Aplastic anaemia, which is a bone marrow disease with a high fatality rate. I was only nine years old at the time and there was nothing I could do to help him. So that frustration really sat with me as I grew up. I found that I was able to bring one little boy, who I had met in hospital, over to America. His name was Sean. I realised that bringing him over and taking him around Disneyland and giving him a ride in a helicopter was the highlight of his brief life. Yet it was so easy for me to do. So I just wanted to do it on a larger scale, and now I'm pleased to say that we grant nearly 2,000 wishes a year. Just recently a little boy from Chicago wanted to meet the Pope, so the local Starlight chapter decided to start by walking into the neighbourhood church and, after much organisation, and faxing the Vatican, he was off on his way to meet the Pope.

ADMIRE:
Peter Ustinov. I think Peter is the most brilliant, nice, kind, funny person that I've ever worked with. I was so impressed by his professionalism and his kindness.

GREATEST MOMENT:
Getting married.

HOLIDAYS:

The most interesting vacation was my trip to the Galapagos Islands, cruising around the islands and meeting the wildlife. It really is an extraordinary place.

FOOD:

Cereal. I like Weetabix, Shredded Wheat and Cornflakes.

MUSIC:

I have a varied taste in music, from Beethoven and Mozart to Wilson Phillips, Whitney Houston and Janet Jackson.

HOBBIES:

I like to restore and re-finish antiques. I have a workshop set up in my garage.

AMBITION:

To just be able to keep working. My career is a job and no more than that. It's a means to support myself, it's not a lifestyle.

HATES:

Bigotry. It comes from stupidity and ignorance.

FIRST KISS:

I think I cut myself on my braces!

ROMANTIC EXPERIENCE:
Meeting my husband Bansi Nagji. My brother introduced us.

PHILLIP SCHOFIELD

FULL NAME:
Phillip Bryan Schofield. My dad's name is Bryan.

NICKNAME:
I have in the past been called Flipper but I've no idea why.

BORN:
I was born on 1 April 1962 at Boundary Park Hospital, Oldham, Lancashire. It was Mother's Day and it was snowing. My birthday now falls on Mother's Day every eleven years. I'm an April Fool by two hours, which my mum desperately tried to avoid! She asked the nurse to amend my time of birth by two

hours – but she said no. But I'm delighted she didn't. It's given me a lot of fun over the years – the great thing is that you never get caught out on April Fool's Day yourself! I'm always pulling off stunts. I got a friend of mine to ring up my management, Peter Powell and Russ Lindsay, pretending to be from Proctor and Gamble, the big advertising agency. He offered a fortune for me to plug a Phillip Schofield Soap-On-A-Rope! They fell for it hook, line and sinker and threw a big party for me, as they worked out how to spend their money. At the end of the night I told them – they were devastated!

SCHOOL:
Trevance Infant's School, then Edgcombe Avenue Middle School and Newquay Pretherran Senior School. I grew up in Cornwall. My first day, I put all the uniform on, had a good time and enjoyed myself. Then, the second day, my mother tried to get me ready and I refused, saying I'd been there once and that was enough. I was a terrible pupil to start with – the teacher actually sent me home at one stage because I was too uncontrollable! I once made a little device which involved fuse wire, tin foil, wax and magnesium ribbon, which when placed in a strategic position caused a very loud bang and a brilliant white light – I thoroughly enjoyed that. I fought the school bully,

who had a giant bullying family. But I did OK and he treated me with respect after that. I know his name but he still has a giant family! I ended up with six O levels.

JOBS:

I used to make candy floss – I was the world's worst. I got fired after about three weeks because I ended up spraying floss over the customers and my boss, who was not amused. It took me ages to walk home with floss sticking all over me. I also used to work in an ice-cream kiosk, which was a nightmare. People are so incredibly rude to you when they are on holiday. Every morning, I would slam a can of coke and leave it on the side. Then, when any particularly obnoxious git was rude, I'd give him the coke can and it would explode in his face. It was good fun getting revenge.

CAREER:

I was a bookings clerk in sport and outside broadcasts at Broadcasting House, I was paid £4,500 a year. Not very much! I ended up working with those same guys on a Radio One Roadshow years later, which was amazing. We drank huge amounts of real ale for two years, until my dad said he was moving to New Zealand and I decided to go with them. I was 19 and didn't want to go because my career was just taking off. But, after six months there, I knew I had made the right decision. My first programme there was *Shazam*, a weekly pop show. It was the perfect place to start – so open and friendly. Incredibly enjoyable. I felt very guilty about leaving in 1985.

FRIGHTENING MOMENT:

I think the first time I was link man on afternoon TV. We started at ten past four and, by about three o'clock, I was shaking with nerves on the fire escape thinking, 'If this goes wrong, my career is over. This is the big time.' Then *Blue Peter* came off three-and-a-half minutes early and I had to start by ad-libbing to a huge picture of Simon Groom with a giant sea-slug! I started quite calm and ended covered in sweat. But I got through it OK. They were great days, though.

I was also racing a mini car, which caught fire when someone ran into it. I was strapped in and couldn't get out – it was terrifying. It took a long time to get me out. I remember making a film with the Red Arrows for *Going Live* about three years ago. I was in the lead plane of nine, which set off down the runway. And the plane right behind us hit the deck and exploded. He ejected out, thank God, and got away with no injuries.

GREATEST MOMENT:

I think it was producing the 1984 *New Zealand Music Awards*. It was my first big show and it really got me on my way. It worked very well. I think meeting Jack Nicholson would be a great moment too. I've met a lot of stars but he meant something special. Also doing the Radio One Roadshow from my hometown of Newquay. It was my greatest ambition and it was wonderful. All the family were there – and I remember being there myself years ago thinking, 'If only...'

COCK-UP:

This was doing an afternoon link-up when absolutely everything went wrong. For the last minute, there was just a series of shots of tapes and God knows what else. When I finally got myself back in vision, I cut the sound out. It was a Friday evening and we couldn't apologise until Monday. All I could hear was my producer saying, 'Sorry, Phil, love, there's nothing we can do!' Fortunately, my boss, Malcolm Walker, walked in afterwards, when I thought I was going to get fired, and roared with laughter saying, 'What wonderful telly – it was a nightmare but I loved it.' Because the boss was laughing, we all started laughing.

CARS:

First one was a Sunbeam Rapier, metallic blue. I was heartbroken when I had to sell it because I couldn't afford to keep it on the road. Now I drive a BMW 325i convertible, which I've had for two years.

HOME:

First property I purchased was a one-bedroom flat in Ealing, West London. Now I live in West London.

HOLIDAYS:

I loved the Seychelles. I'm quite happy anywhere with sunshine.

FOOD:

American soft shell crabs, which I get in a little restaurant up the road from me. You eat the whole thing, the claws, the shell, everything. You eat them with garlic and almonds. If they don't have them on the menu, I don't go in. My favourite restaurants are a Thai place near me and the Langham Hilton, which is like going back in time.

DRINK:

Jack Daniels and orange juice, but not too much orange. I'm also a great supporter of New Zealand wine. I've slept in offices, I've slept in tubes – I've had some terrible nights on booze. The worst one recently was Peter Powell's stag night. It was a wild, crazy night. There was also an outrageous Toga party a few years back, a mile from where I live and I don't know to this day how I got back. What amazes me is how I get my contact lenses out every time – I always wake up with them out, however drunk I was the night before.

MUSIC:
In the car at the moment, there is REM, Deacon Blue, and Hue and Cry. I used to love Then Jericho. My favourite album would be *Love Over Gold* by Dire Straits, for the memories it gives me of a great evening I spent with a woman. I'm not telling you any more about her, but it was wonderful. My first record was Nielsen's 'Without You'.

BOOK:
Stark by Ben Elton.

ADMIRE:
I am not impressed by great people so much as rebels, who do all the stuff that I can't do. I would love to be as bad as James Dean or a young Marlon Brando. I would also like to be as observant as Ben Elton and Billy Connolly and as cool as Sean Connery.

HEIGHT:
5ft 11in.

HOBBIES:
Scuba diving – I can't do it enough.

FILM:
Local Hero or *Dead Poets Society*.

AMBITION:
To go into space. Not on one of those commercial trips but actually on a rocket. It must be the most fantastic experience.

WORST EXPERIENCE:
My dad's heart attack. We were all in the lounge of our New Zealand house about eight years ago and he just dropped like a stone. The worst experience I've ever had. Even now, I can't watch heart attacks on movies or TV without becoming very emotional. I had, amazingly, picked up the rudiments of first aid and, perhaps by divine intervention, it all came back to me. The ambulance men gave me a certificate saying I had saved a life that night. I just jumped on Dad. We are such a close family and to see the fabric of our family disappearing before my eyes was just terrible. Mum was distraught and didn't know what to do. When Dad came round, he couldn't remember anything. I actually beat the ambulance to the hospital because I was so worried. I'd been whacking him so hard I burst a blood vessel in my hand and bruised my arms. The only thing that hurt him afterwards was his chest, where I had hit him. It's a

very emotional thing for us – we both know what happened. I had given Dad three minutes' massage and I was planning to electric-shock him with the wire from a reading lamp, which is so dangerous. But that's what goes through your mind. He was out for two minutes until I brought him round. He lost his sense of smell and taste for a year afterwards. I think it was his diet that caused it – too many steaks. First thing Dad heard when he came round was a guy on the radio saying, 'There's no reason why anyone should die of a heart attack...' Ever since, he has been a vegan. He is 56 now and fit as a fiddle.

FANCY:
Demi Moore for a very long time. I was one of the originals – way before *Ghost*. We discovered her stunning looks in *Blame It On Rio*. There is lusting fantasy, when it's purely sexual, and that is Demi's attraction for me. But I really fancied Whoopi Goldberg, because she made me laugh. I could imagine having a relationship with her, but not Demi. Also Julia Roberts and Meg Ryan. I am very fickle.

FIRST KISS:
She was called Susan, it was in a Wendy House at my infant's school. I was five and it was a stolen kiss. My

first real kiss was with a girl called Jackie, who I went out with for a long time when I was 14.

FIRST BONK:

No one forgets, do they? It was in the sand dunes in Newquay. I was about 15 and I took my flipflops off as a boy and put them on again as a man. I remember her well – and her name began with an L, that's all I am saying. I still see her occasionally and don't want to embarrass her. She knows she was my first!

CHRIS TARRANT

NICKNAME:
Chrissy Wissy at Capital Radio where I do the
weekday breakfast show. When I was a snotty little
school kid in Reading, they used to call me Cuthbert.

BORN:
10 October 1946. I am a Libra, the sign of balance
and sensitivity. I was born in Reading. My father's
name is Basil and my mother is Joan. I have no
brothers or sisters.

SCHOOL:
My first school was a twee little private school called
'Number Nine' in Reading. It was a private house

turned into a school, with chickens running around the playground. I went to look at it six years ago with my girlfriend but there was nothing there, just a pile of bricks between number seven and number eleven. My next school was called Worcester. It was a minor public school, where I seemed to spend all my time being caned. I used to get caned every day as far as I can remember. I would get things like twelve of the best in front of the whole school. It was usually for sneaking out of school after hours and meeting girls from the nearest girls' boarding school, which was even more repressed than ours. It was run by a Miss Molest, funnily enough. We used to get into fights out of school. We were usually chased by the local yobs, who didn't like silly public schoolboys.

FRIGHTENING MOMENT:
Me and a friend of mine called Andrews decided we would try out a canoe we had bought for a quid at school, when we were about fourteen. We took it straight out on the weir in Worcester, which was madness, us in this tiny unstable canoe. We went straight into this swirling stuff at incredible speed. God knows how we got out of that alive. When I was in the scouts doing swimming training, I got swept out to sea. For some reason, in his infinite wisdom, the scoutmaster decided we ought to swim in the

estuary of the River Ax, where it goes pouring down to the sea. It's got a vicious current. We were doing these floating exercises and, before we knew it, all 30 of us were miles away from the beach and there were kids all round me panicking and screaming. People came rushing out to rescue us in boats. Three of us were rescued by a fishing boat, and a friend of mine, called Tubby, was lying in the bottom of the boat all covered in froth which had come up from his lungs. The fisherman said to us, 'He's gone, that one – he's dead.' Luckily, he wasn't. I remember being very frightened, if they had got to us any later we would all have been gonners.

UNIVERSITY:
Birmingham. I did a very strange course and got a bluffers degree in English.

JOBS:
Driving lorries. Actually, the happiest days of my working life. Every morning I'd just load up this enormous lorry with lawnmowers and drive them from Reading to Liverpool, Sheffield, Edinburgh and so on. I was built like a brickhouse. I must have been the fittest I've ever been in my life. I always used to say, if anything went desperately wrong in my career, I'd go back to lorry driving. I suspect I wouldn't now.

Then I did a series of odd jobs, I was a night security man for a while for Securicor. I was more scared of the guard dogs than the burglars. You used to have to ring in every hour. They'd say, 'Security of the nation,' and we'd have to reply, 'Vigilant and valiant here,' and if you dozed off for five minutes the place would be full of police. The trouble was the dogs used to go mental every time the phone rang. My teaching days were pretty rough. I used to teach in East London, a class called the Easter Leavers in New Cross. They were mainly oversized skinheads and hardnuts who didn't know what a full stop was. There were meant to be 40 to a class but you were lucky if 20 turned up. Sadly, most of us used to turn a blind eye to truancy.

HOME:
It was during that period that I used to live in the back of a Mini-van, registration 161 GLO. I had been living with a girl in Fulham. We'd had this almighty row at one in the morning, so I said I was off. The trouble was I'd got a mile down the road and suddenly realised I had nowhere to live. So I slept that night in the van and then the next night, and found I quite liked it, and I ended up spending the next six months living in the van. It was difficult with girls, because they'd say can I come back to your place and I'd say, 'Well actually

you're in it!' If they wanted coffee, they'd have to make it on a Calor gas stove, between their knees! I used to park it outside the school and the kids used to wake me up: 'Morning, Mr Tarrant, it's eight-thirty.' The greatest thing for me was I actually got mail delivered to me in the van. The postie would hand me mail addressed to 161 GLO (grey Mini-van) Sprawls Road, London SE3.

CAREER:

I joined the Central Office of Information, for two-and-a-half years, where I got my director's ticket. But I soon realised I was not destined to be a Steven Spielberg, unfortunately, so I wrote this very brash letter, saying things like: 'I am the face of the seventies, and this is your last chance to snap me up.' To their credit, most of the TV stations I had written to threw it in the bin, but ATV offered me a week on the six o'clock magazine show. I ended up reading the news with very long hair and a Harry Fenton suit. Then *Tiswas* came along and I'd get 25 quid for three hours on a Saturday morning. For the next seven years, Lenny Henry, Sally, John and all the team used to throw vast amounts of water over audiences and stick flans in any unsuspecting person's face.

Then came *OTT*, which I produced as well. But I spent most of the time dodging the flack and complaints from the IBA and other political bodies. Then I did a chat show with Jimmy Greaves on Friday nights. Then I went to the BBC.

KIDS:
I've got three and we are arranging to have more. For me, they're the greatest thing, they keep your feet on the ground.

HOBBIES:
Catching big fish. I've always got my tackle in the boot of my car and it's not unusual for me to come straight to work on the breakfast show from a night fishing, clanking a huge bucket of fish up the stairs and into the studio.

COCK-UP:
In 1980, on *OTT*, a famous girl was on the show playing a game where you had to remove an article of clothing every time you got a wrong answer, and she forgot to mention she wasn't wearing a bra. The first article she took off was her T-shirt...

CARS:
First was a green Standard van, which cost me £120. Now I have a red Mercedes 300 SE.

HOME:
A house on the river in Cobham, Surrey.

HOLIDAYS:
Africa. I'm going back there again and I'm going to Alaska this summer to live among Eskimos. Last year I went off to the airport and found I had left my passport on top of the car before driving off.

FOOD:
I love Greek nights out, smashing the plates and so on.

DRINK:
I used to drink whisky, but I found it used to make me go most peculiar so I tend to drink much more beer than I used to.

MUSIC:
I'm a big Status Quo fan. At their recent anniversary gig at Butlins in Minehead, where Quo had performed their very first gig together, they invited me up on to the stage and sang Happy Birthday to me.

FIRST RECORD:
'Apache' by The Shadows. I used to play it on my little Dansette minor.

BOOKS:
My favourite was *Silence of the Lambs*. I couldn't put it down. I was actually reading it while the records were going round on the show.

FAVOURITE SINGER:
Chris Rea.

HEIGHT:
6ft 2in.

BIGGEST FISH CAUGHT:
105lb sailfish off the Seychelles last year.

FILM:
Un Homme Et Une Femme.

ADMIRES:
Michael Jackson.

AMBITION:
Stop working, and start enjoying the rest of my life.

HATES:
Madonna, journalists, estate agents, wheel-clampers, traffic wardens.

FANCY:
Sigourney Weaver.

FIRST KISS:
A girl called Jackie in Reading, when I was nine. We were playing postman's knock and I had about 27 kisses.

FIRST BONK:
I was quite young. It was a heterosexual experience. I can't tell you her name because the person is still around today and not a million miles away from my everyday life, and it would be terribly embarrassing.

ANTHEA TURNER

FULL NAME:
Anthea Turner.

NICKNAME:
A-T, Mop-head or Lil.

BORN:
25 May 1961. Stoke-On-Trent, Staffordshire. I'm a Gemini.

SCHOOL:
I went to Norton County Primary School, Holden Lane Comprehensive and St Dominic's Grammar School. My worst school memory was the entire time

I spent at Holden Lane Comp – it was terrible. And my favourite memory was St Dominic's because it was such a relief to be somewhere else.

JOBS:
My first real job was working for the AA's breakdown and information department.

CAREER:
I became a walking oracle on where Stoke-On-Trent Council were digging holes and diverting traffic, then broadcast the information to frustrated motorists via BBC local radio.

FRIGHTENING MOMENT:
Watching the BBC World revolving and then hearing that great voice of authority say, 'And now, over to Children's BBC for but first this with Anthea Turner.' It was a case of GULP! There's no turning back.

GREATEST MOMENT:
My wedding day. I believe it is every girl's fantasy to walk down the aisle in a beautiful dress and to see the man of their dreams waiting for them, and that's how it was for me. I only wish I'd known how quickly the day goes and how important it is to

savour each moment. I wish I'd videotaped it now so we could play it back again and again. And I remember the day in May 1989, when I had been booked by *Blue Peter* to be a guest on their programme. Arriving at Television Centre, I was ready with every grin, smile and persuasive line I knew to get my car into the grounds. I needed none of it. The security patrolman greeted me with a welcoming smile and the words: 'Go through, Anthea, and pop your car up by reception.' It was the day I really knew my career had begun.

COCK-UP:

I once took the BBC's Signal Radio outside broadcast unit, consisting of a Range Rover and 21ft trailer, to a Round Table summer carnival. With help, I parked the monster in a field and set about my job, which was great until a member of the *Coronation Street* cast used our stage to hold an autograph-signing session. With all the extra weight on the front, coupled with the legs being placed on nothing but crusty cowpats, the whole lot, with me at the helm, lurched forward – throwing people and equipment everywhere.

CARS:

My first was a Mini called Champagne Charlie – now I drive a Golf GTi.

HOLIDAYS:
Speaking as a true Gemini, I love equally different types, from a crash-out in the Caribbean or Med to a fresh air and sensible clothes touring holiday.

FOOD:
As national dishes go, I love Italian food. But a ritual I carry out four times a year consists of munching a plate of homemade chips and Heinz baked beans with salt and vinegar, plus at least two slices of white bread with lashings of butter, all washed down with a glass of full-cream milk. It's a real treat.

DRINK:
Guinness or Ribena.

MUSIC:
Difficult to pin down. But largely anything that has been well crafted, from U2 to a good pop record. At the moment, my favourite is Chesney Hawks's 'The One And Only.'

BOOK:
An atlas.

HOBBIES:
Keep fit and horse-riding.

ADMIRE:
Real flesh and blood people from any walk of life.

HEIGHT:
5ft 6in.

FILM:
Dances With Wolves was the last movie to really affect me.

FRIGHTENING EXPERIENCE:
Being involved in a motorbike stunt that went horribly wrong during a live television show of the Royal Tournament. I was hit by a blazing bike and my face was badly burned – I lost the top two layers of skin and my eyebrows and eyelashes were frazzled. I never thought I would look the same again, but my skin healed amazingly quickly.

FANCY:
My husband Peter Powell – would you like to throw up now or later? I used to collect posters of Peter when he was a Radio One DJ and put them on my bedroom wall. We finally met in a lift at Broadcasting House but I lost my nerve and didn't say a word. Then Peter became my manager and we slowly grew together.

FIRST KISS:

I had practised for some time on the back of my hand while gazing at a poster of David Cassidy. So I was fully prepared for everything except bad breath... I can't tell you who it was.

ERNIE WISE

NAME:
Ernest Wiseman.

NICKNAME:
Eric used to call me Short, Fat Hairy Legs and My Little Fat Friend. Jack Hilton, the bandleader, shortened my name to Ernie, because he thought it was too long for showbiz.

BORN:
27 November 1925. I am sick to death of jokes about bus-passes. I was born in Armley, Leeds. Harry and Convie were Mum and Dad. I have a

brother Gordon and sisters Ann and Constance. My younger brother Edward died.

SCHOOL:
Fitzwilliam School in Hemsworth. I didn't like school. I loved my first teacher, Miss Dott, but I wasn't a great learner. My favourite subject was history. I remember breaking my arm jumping from a bench to swing on a tree like Tarzan.

JOBS:
When I was very young, I began to perform with my father – we did a double act around the working men's clubs called Carson and Kid. I was eight and we earned three pounds fifty a weekend – more than he earned in a week on the railway. When I was 12, I did an audition for the *Big Discovery* show. I went on that night at the Prince's Theatre, now the Shaftesbury Theatre, and I was an overnight success. After that, I went on tour earning six pounds a week. I stayed with Jack Hilton and lived like a rich prince. Then, when all the theatres opened up, I joined *You Takes A Bow* and met Eric. He was a bit younger than me, but I remember he sang a song called, appropriately, 'I'm Not All There' when he auditioned for Jack. Our double act started soon afterwards. We used to share a double

bed together on tour to save money. In those days, nobody gave it a second thought. But he used to snore terribly and I couldn't get any sleep. So one night I gave him a big kiss and HE didn't sleep a wink!

FRIGHTENING MOMENT:

When I got a 1 a.m. phone call in Wakefield to hear Eric had had a heart attack. That was the first one in 1968, and it was a big shock. We performed on stage together again a few weeks later and I honestly didn't know if he was going to collapse on stage and die. So that's when we decided to stop doing live stuff and play safe in the studio.

GREATEST MOMENT:

Appearing on *The Ed Sullivan Show*, doing The Royal Command Performances, and playing at the London Palladium.

COCK-UP:

We were doing *Sleeping Beauty* in panto up in Manchester and doing fantastic business. Then we were asked to go to the Palladium for a show and we didn't want to do it. We were tired and the show went totally wrong. As we walked off, Eric said it was the worst f******* show we had ever done. But he forgot he still had his mike on and the whole audience heard it... and nodded! It was a disaster.

CARS:

The first one was a builder's truck that Eric and I bought in Llanelli for £190. It kept breaking down – totally useless. Then I got a new Triumph Mayflower. Now I have got a Rolls-Royce, a Jaguar and a Mercedes Sports, which is a super car because it stops so well. They are the best cars financially and mechanically that I can imagine buying.

HOME:

First home was in East Ardsley, near Wakefield. Now I live in Maidenhead, on the river. It's Hollywood-on-Thames. I have a boat called *Lady Doreen II*, a swimming pool and a tennis court.

HOLIDAYS:

I go to Lauderhill, in Florida, where I own a condominium.

FOOD:

I like English food best, a steak or a Dover sole. Then French second, then Chinese and Italian and Indian definitely last – twice a year at the most.

DRINK:

I have always loved an American dry Martini, shaken not stirred of course – and preferably in New York.

MUSIC:

I like swing, big band music. Glenn Miller's 'Pennsylvania 6500' was my first record. I loved Count Basie, Duke Ellington and the Woody Herman band, who I actually met once in America.

BOOKS:

The 1914–18 War fascinates me. And biographies, I like to know what went on in all the stars' private lives. I love the gossip – everything about them. I have a marvellous collection. What intrigues me is how so many women were exploited by men.

HEIGHT:

5ft 5in.

HOBBIES:

I am interested in money – finance. I dabble in the stock market, though it's a bit dicey at the moment. I am not a gambler, just safe stuff mainly. My portfolio has gone down by about 25 per cent like most people's.

FILMS:

All the old musicals. *Singing In The Rain* was the best ever made. Fred Astaire and Gene Kelly were my favourites. Kelly wrote to me once, saying he loved my version of *Singing In The Rain*! Can you believe that?

ADMIRE:

Mickey Rooney I loved – he was a wonderful performer with a very hectic private life. In comedy, I didn't like Chaplin or Keaton – I preferred the Bob Hope style. Of today's crop, I like Russ Abbot – he's the one the public like. But the others are too shocking for me, they talk about subjects I find embarrassing, probably because of my age. But I did like the *Blackadder* series in the trenches. There was a good message there, as well as comedy.

AMBITION:

I try to stay away from too much stress. But I regret I never made a Hollywood picture and never appeared on Broadway – the ultimate in showbiz is America as far as I am concerned. If we had succeeded in the States, we would have done a lot better but it doesn't matter now!

HATES:

I don't like today's music and the lowering of standards. I am very anti-violence and very anti-sex. I hate the stuff that's going on now. Our society is in a terrible state.

FANCY:

In the old days, I loved Eleanor Powell, a wonderful tap dancer. I still love Glenda Jackson, my favourite.

FIRST KISS:

I don't really remember, to be honest. But it may have been a schoolteacher.

TERRY WOGAN

FULL NAME:
Michael Terence Wogan.

NICKNAME:
I am called Terry because my father's name was Terence and we wanted to avoid confusion in our little home. Everyone in Limerick calls me Bawkey, but I don't know why. The leader of the gang I was in made them up as he went along and Bawkey was mine. I regret that I never had a stage name. I would have done, if I had known I was going to be famous. It's been a lumber for my children, who now have to put up with being a Wogan.

BORN:
3 August 1938.

GREATEST MOMENT:
I will never forget a BBC cameraman who went to Berlin as the wall came down and came back with a picture of the wall for me. It has 'Thankyou Reagan' crossed out, 'Thankyou Gorby' crossed out, and 'Thankyou Wogan' put in. He swears he didn't do it himself – and I've got that photo everywhere at home! Meeting James Stewart was another highlight – what a lovely, gentle man. He loved everything about Hollywood – he never saw any badness about anyone. Kirk Douglas, too, was fantastic, though he was much more abrasive. Bette Davis was a fiendish bitch, always has been. But stars like her deliver the goods – that's their tradition. Some actors have very little brain of course, which doesn't help. And why should people like Jane Fonda be allowed to spout off about political affairs – who is she to do that? She has behaved like a marionette for everyone she's been married to. When she married Roger Vadim, she was a striptease artist. Now she likes news and current affairs because she's seeing Ted Turner...

COCK-UP:
George Best was the great embarrassment. We

watched him all day because of his reputation. He came here reasonably sober and, after 15 minutes in hospitality, he was in great form. But then he came on drunk. I could see he was gone, razzled, absolutely elephants. I thought about taking him off. But he may have turned into a nasty drunk and started to f and blind as he was dragged off the stage. The least harmful thing was to let him stay on. Anne Bancroft was terrible too – she didn't know it was a live show and she was just terrified. You could hear her counting to herself as she walked on, because she was so scared. She was literally shivering with fear. We also have people who try the nose candy – they go into the loo before the show and we know what's going on. They either come on three feet off the ground or saying things with a knowing look in their eye. There is one comedian, who I admire enormously, who does it – he just smiles his way through each time he's on. I can spot it when it happens. The stars literally leap towards me.

CARS:

My first car was a second-hand black Morris Minor, which my father bought for me for £150. I met my wife in that one. Since then, I've had so many cars – a Raleigh Elf, a Sunbeam Rapier, an EType Jag, a couple of Lancias, a Lotus Eclat, a Rolls-Royce, a Mercedes and now I have a Bentley 8. Funny thing is that I'm useless mechanically.

HOME:

I moved out of Bray 17 years ago when Michael Parkinson moved next door. I could see the area declining immediately. Now I live in Taplow.

HOLIDAYS:

I have a house on the southeast coast of Spain and we have great fun there. We've been going for seven years, and my kids all speak Spanish now.

FOOD:

Helen's a terrific cook, particularly potatoes. My mum's dreadful though! One of my sons is now studying to be a chef, which is wonderful because I like eating – there's nothing better than nice food and long lunches. My favourite food is caviar and foie gras.

DRINK:

I used to drink a lot of vodka and I still get tempted to go back on the vodkas and lemonades occasionally. But now I usually stick to wine.

MUSIC:

I have no knowledge of pop music now. I hear INXS at

home and watch *Top Of The Pops*, but I just don't know who's in the charts or who's in what band. I don't know how someone like Simon Bates does it. In the car, I listen to classical music.

BOOK:

A P. G. Woodhouse anthology and *Bonfire of the Vanities*.

FILM:

High Society is the film I've seen the most. Grace Kelly was just fabulous and it had everyone in it – Crosby, Sinatra. A magical film.

HEIGHT:

6ft.

HOBBIES:

I am pretty lazy. I ski with the family, but after three days I'm bored witless. I play tennis, and golf once a month off a 16 handicap.

AMBITION:

At this stage, I have gone as far as I can go in TV, with a three-times-a-week chat show. I've done it for six years now and I think there will be a lot more chat shows and hosts, because that is what people want. They want easy-to-watch game shows and talk shows. It was an enormous risk doing the show but I wanted to do it. I wanted to create the intimacy of a radio format. They said I wouldn't last six weeks but I have. I try to make people feel they are really there with me. I suppose I do sometimes think, 'What the hell am I doing here now?' Everyone does, including George Bush, probably. I wanted to be famous and I like having money and getting restaurant tables. But I would like NOT to be found standing on the beach when the tide's gone out. I've always left people wanting more and I am now seriously considering an alternative. I've always wanted to be the best, I think you have to be. I couldn't be a backroom boy, I've been too spoiled by what I've done. The BBC still thinks people are in the Dark Ages, still need to be protected from camera shots of guests leaving... everyone knows what happens, why don't we show it? Eamonn Andrews always said you go when the people at the top decide you are passe, or the public are bored, or if you are fed up with it. But I don't want to get stuck doing the same thing. I'd like to go back into radio. I would like to work in America, but I've wasted 18 months out there when we could have all made our decisions in two weeks. It had nothing to do with money. Nobody except Benny Hill has ever made it in the States. It's the biggest market in the world. But I think maybe I am too old.

FIRST KISS:

It was in Kilkee, County Clare, a bumbling, stumbling affair. I was about 15 and she was an older woman. You didn't get much of a chance where I came from. It was raining and on the cliffs and a bumping of teeth. It was a hopeless, stupid affair. I think her name was Betty.

STEVE WRIGHT

FULL NAME:
Stephen Richard Wright.

NICKNAME:
I was called Captain Zero years ago, because I worked in insurance and used to rush around everywhere at 40mph.

BORN:
26 August 1954 in Greenwich, London. I'm a Virgo but I don't believe in all that stuff really. I had asthma badly as a kid and was in an oxygen tent in hospital on and off for eight years.

SCHOOLS:

Edmund Waller School in New Cross, South London. Merlin Rise in Epsom, Surrey. Prince Avenue School in Southend-On-Sea. I was always organising things, from the school paper to the local hospital radio station. I was always in trouble for talking. I was caned ten times for chatting in class. I wasn't wildly naughty, I just couldn't shut up. They slippered me once a month but it wasn't much of a deterrent, as you can see! In fact, I grew to quite like it! I got three O levels in maths, physics and woodwork.

JOBS:

I left school at 18 and became a British Telecom Engineer. It lasted five months, until they told me I would have to start climbing up telegraph poles and I wasn't very keen on that. I wanted to work in the exchange because I liked electronics and stuff, but it wasn't to be. Then I joined an insurance company called Willis Faber, then Black Sea and Baltic. I used to talk about hull damage all day for three years. I left that to join a local paper called the *Ilford Pictorial*, then the *Evening Echo* and the *Berkshire Chronicle*. I was a good journalist, a very good journalist. In fact, I am a better journalist than I am broadcaster.

CAREER:

My first radio job was with LBC, in London, writing news copy. I used to read the stories out and a guy called Neil French-Blake heard me and he offered me a job on Thames Valley radio as a disc jockey. I'd never even thought of that – the whole idea is still absurd. I was fired twice from that station – once for insulting the Dutch royal family, while one of them was actually listening, and the other time for playing the wrong day's adverts. I played Sunday's on Saturday. I was reinstated both times. I moved on to Radio Luxembourg for nine months, which was a nightmare. I hated it because they loathed the Brits there at the time, because of something to do with the war. I tried to explain that I had nothing to do with it. But they weren't having any of that. They were openly hostile. Then Radio One offered me a job on Saturday night, 7.30 p.m. to 10 p.m. I took it because I was missing Rich Tea biscuits and the *Sun*. It wasn't a great slot but I liked it. I was kept off the daytime slot for three years and I thought I was going to be fired by the end. All the ideas that are now in my show were rejected at the time for being too out of the ordinary. I was considering going back to papers or moving abroad. Then the present controller, Johnny Beerling, took over and I was given my chance. I still get in to trouble now for a lot of things but I get away with them.

FRIGHTENING MOMENT:

Interviewing Prime Minister John Major at No 10 Downing Street. I didn't know what he was like or whether it was going to happen or not. I was out of my environment and felt very nervous about making a big balls-up of it. But he took me seriously and I ended up feeling like Brian Walden. One funny moment was when I took some Paracetemol pills from his desk, because I had a headache, and he told me they were his pills – and I'd just finished the bottle. But he laughed and said he could get some more. He was quite a serious, sincere and honest man. I wouldn't go as far as saying he is boring but he does have some catching up to do in the charisma stakes.

GREATEST MOMENT:

Meeting Simon Bates, a man who everyone is in awe of. When Bates knows you exist, that has to be your greatest moment, doesn't it ? No, seriously, the single best moment was when my wife said she would marry me in 1985. I was doing the afternoon show and I asked her to marry me on the air. She was a reporter on TVS and heard me proposing as she drove to work that evening. She had no mobile phone and was on the motorway, so she called up via an AA phone box on the hard shoulder and said yeah! That was brilliant, and another true story.

COCK-UP:

I threw up on air when I was on Thames Valley Radio 210. This guy came on and talked about de-worming a dog. He was so dull and ended up saying you had to put your hand up its backside and pull out the stuff inside, and throw away the worms. He was describing it all in graphic detail while I was eating this Cornish pasty and I started feeling queasy. Eventually, I just threw up everywhere. It was disgusting. I had to explain to the listeners what happened and I didn't have him in again.

CARS:

My first was a green Hillman Imp, which cost me £70 and lasted nine months until it conked out and I took it sadly to the scrap heap. Now I drive a Renault 5, which my wife bought.

HOME:

My first place was a one-bedroomed studio flat in Ladbroke Grove, London. It was pokey but adequate. Now I live in Henley-on-Thames. My neighbours include George Harrison, Bjorn from Abba and George Cole but I haven't met any of them.

HOLIDAYS:

Los Angeles – it's such a great relief to go somewhere you can meet so many shallow people in one place.

FOOD:

Italian – my favourite restaurant is Quo Vadis in Soho, London. It's fantastic there.

DRINK:

I have never drunk very much. A little Tia Maria or rum and black. I don't like the taste of alcohol much – I prefer coke to be honest and ten cups of coffee every day.

MUSIC:

I'm a big fan of New Age stuff like Rick Wakeman's new album. I love the rave culture – KLF and EMF. I have some classical music, which I enjoy, and urban rap is superb. Guys like Ice-T will be looked back on in 50 years' time as poets – the Keats of their time. My favourite all-time artist would have to be someone like Paul McCartney. OK, he's off the boil at the moment but look at what the man's done – it's phenomenal.

BOOK:

Stark by Ben Elton would have to be one.

ADMIRE:
Mother Teresa, President Bush [Editor's note: George Bush Senior], – who I think is a man of integrity. The Pope [John Paul II] seems like a good old boy and professionally Terry Wogan, who has a good attitude. Also anybody who really kicks a bit or arse, like Peter O'Toole and Ben Elton.

HEIGHT:
5ft 9in.

HOBBIES:
Photography, collecting old radios, electronics and travel. Now I am collecting antiques, especially Georgian furniture.

FILM:
Some Like It Hot and *Annie Hall*.

AMBITION:
To stay happy, and I would like to go into stock-markets and that line of work. I'm not that interested in TV really.

FRIGHTENING EXPERIENCE:
I was on an 80-Beater propeller plane from Brussels to Luxembourg, a short hop. One of the engines had

packed up and the other one was about to, so we had to make an emergency landing in a field. The trouble was that there were a load of trees in the way. The captain made an announcement which ended with the words: 'I hope we can pull up before the trees.' I braced myself to crash, and prayed I would be thrown clear. It was like the *Airplane* movies – everyone was screaming. But, when we were literally a foot from the ground, the engine started up again and we took off. The pilot was a hero.

FANCY:
My wife Cyndy.

FIRST KISS:
A girl called Janice Ridgeway in a shed in Cricklewell, Essex. We were both eight and we were at school together. It was a memorable experience for me but I haven't seen her for 30 years so it can't have been for her!

FIRST BONK:
My mind has suddenly gone a complete blank...